FA

From the
LAZY BEE

Featuring Americana Basics
from the
Northwest Mountains

By Jo Ann Bender
F.C. "Bud" Budinger

Published by Bender & Associates
COLVILLE WA

Dear Gracious Reader:

Come into my kitchen. Make yourself at home. Would you like a cup of tea? There's water brewing in a copper antique pot on the wood stove. Maybe a slice of walnut bread to go with it? On your way here, did you see wild life? Turkeys? A bull elk? Bear cubs in a tree? A bald eagle on a fence post?

Why do we call it the Lazy Bee when, from all you can see on our fifteen acres, that it's obvious we aren't lazy? In fact, some say that we like to build and create so much that they wouldn't be surprised if we don't build all the way down to the pond.

The joy of living so close to this forested land does, as Thoreau says about Walden Pond, drive life into a corner and suck out the marrow of its meaning.

We aren't so busy that husband Bud. . . engineer, writer about the NW Indian wars in 1858, and volunteer fireman. . . can't take time to talk to a chubby skunk who waddles through his barn leaving him unharmed. Or, if Bud's repairing a tractor in the barnyard and a white rabbit comes by, he'll see him munching the new spring grass. When the rabbit lifts his head, Bud will talk to him. The rabbit will listen to Bud awhile before moving on.

Whatever is going on at the Lazy Bee, I carve out time from bringing in the wood for our stoves, or going on an hour's walk with the neighbors, to write. Whether it's stories accompanying these recipes or a novel, writing is the second most fun for me to do. I'll let you guess what the best might be.

When the first version of this cookbook was published in 1992, I prepared food without running water in a much smaller kitchen. At that time the Lazy Bee was known as *The Cabin*.. And so it continues in the minds of family or friends who came here at a time when this area was less populated and more primitive than it is today .

During those early years, Bud and I also hosted bed and breakfast guests at Hillside House in Spokane. It was an architect-designed ultra -modern house with huge windows that overlooked a terraced and treed lot on the Southhill. It was a home so unlike the Lazy Bee where the setting is designed by Nature, not man.

Our stand of evergreens are 20 percent taller than when we came here twenty years ago. But forests have health problems, too. So we've taken the Washington State University Forest Management class to be better shepherds of their health.

The mountains that surround us are still the same. The nearest ranges are in the shape of sleeping dragons. Wildlife moves about in them on paths through the forests. Mountain roads change as new areas are logged and they lead us to new adventures in the wilderness.

After a hard rain or snowfall, the sky becomes a shade of blue that isn't on paint charts. The clarity of the crystal blue color is visual proof of air that's not polluted.

"Queen of quiet" reins here. You can hear the floor boards in the Tree House room squeak, the screen door that goes bang, the croking of a little green tree frog, the logs snapping in the wood stove.

But, back to these recipes. Many in the first edition were too good to be lost so they're in the last section of this book entitled, Too Good to Be Left Out. Great ones like: Ham on Top Stove, Brunch Egg Casserole, Frozen Fruit Salad, or the simple apple dessert which takes minutes to prepare but looks as if it's taken longer.

Most recipes have few ingredients, ones you probably have on hand. I can't wait to show you how to make a slow-roasted pork that will receive rave reviews, or the oatmeal/apple cookie that Bud likes almost as much as Dorothea's chocolate chip one.

If there ever is another edition of this cookbook, the area may be different. Folks are discovering this 'Forgotten Corner' of Washington State and are coming here to live in record numbers probably because rural areas of nearby Montana and Idaho are too expensive.

But, as I write this, just a trickle of vehicles pass by on Deep Lake Boundary Road.

Baked Cheesecake

I was laying in the hammock, zapped of energy by a persistant cough. Four-year-old granddaughter Frances came rushing over. "Grandma Jo, why are you coughing so hard?" I asked, "Do you have something that can help me stop coughing? Maybe a magic wand that you could wave?" She held up her little finger on the right hand. "Now," I asked, coughing again, "do you have any magic words?" Solomnly, she said, "I love you." The cough melted away. We went in together to dish up some cheesecake.

8 oz. cream cheese, softened
1/2 cup sugar
1 Tbsp. lemon juice
1/4 tsp. vanilla
Dash salt.
2 eggs
1 graham cracker prepared
    crust

Topping:

1 cup sour cream
2 Tbsp. sugar
1/4 tsp. vanilla

Beat cream cheese and 1/2 cup sugar with mixer until fluffy. Beat in lemon juice, 1/4 tsp. vanilla and salt. Add eggs, one at a time, mixing until just combined after each addition Place crust on baking sheet & pour in cream cheese mixture. Bake at 325 about 25 min. until knife inserted l inch from edge comes out clean.

Combine topping. Spread carefully over cheese cake and bake 325 for l0 minutes. Cool l hr. Refrigerate 2 hours. Garnish with berries or a berry sauce.

Baked Garlic

"I'm going to lose my garlic crop." He sounded so heart-broken, his face crestfallen as he explained his dilemnna. "Everyone who told me they'd help with the harvest have backed out." So I asked him to tell me in explicit detail just how the harvesting is done. I listened and said, "I think I can find help for you. In this area, we're a community." To the rescue, Leesa, Judy, Martha, Ellen and Meerilyn came with me up to his garden on the mountain. We worked in teams of two in our raincoats and gloves plucking out the garlic, hauling it in wheel barrows to a working site in the forest. Upon two plywood panels, we washed and cut the plants, then stacked it in his pickup for him to hang to dry. For our efforts we later received his Yukon Gold potatoes, squash and several kinds of garlic.

4 to 8 wholegarlic bulbs

Olive Oil

Slice off the top of each garlic bulb to expose a bit of the flesh.

Arrange in a shallow pan.

Drizzle wtih oilive oil.

Bake about 45 minutes in a 350 degree oven.

Squeeze out the soft pulp to use on bread or meat.

Baked Potato Strips

It was one of those unbelievably gorgeous fall afternoons. We docked our 1954 aluminum boat along the bank of the Columbia River by China Bend Winery. We got out and walked up a path, passed a urt and waved to a barefoot woman sitting on the top step, then walked through the vineyard up to the cluster of the mellow-wooden buildings of the Winery. We saw a white-clad table with marigolds sprinkled down the middle set under the trees on the lush green lawn. We were there to treat Jack and Marva to a lunch made of produce from Victory's garden. The food was so good that our guests insisted upon treating us.

2 lbs. Russet spuds, cut and peeled lengthwise into 1/4 inch strips

1/4 cup corn oil

Kosher salt

Set oven to 450. In a large bowl, put spud strips and cover them cold water. Let stand 20-30 minutes.

Heat two large baking sheets with rims for five minutes in the oven. Drain spuds and pat dry. Put them in a dry bowl, add oil to coat. Spread them out on the hot tins and bake 35 min. or until crispy. Stir occasionally.

Banana Pudding

A question often asked by female visitors is, "Where do you buy groceries?" They must have noticed that there are no stores on the way here. So, we expain that we shop in Canada, which is fifteen miles away. In Colville, that's around fifty minutes, and, Spokane, about two to three hours down the road. For a few dairy or grocery items, we can drive ten minutes to the Waneta Quick Stop. Cooks who live in the country are great list makers. Bananas are always on our grocery list. This recipe makes up quickly and looks great in tall, old-fashioned ice cream dishes.

3 cups cold milk

Pour milk into large bowl. Add dry pudding mix and beat for 2 minutes until well blended.

2 small packages vanilla instant pudding

30 crushed cookies or wafers

Put the crushed wafers or cookies at the bottom of the dish. Add layers of the sliced bananas pudding and crushed wafers. Repeat again.

3 medium bananas, sliced

Whipped topping or whipped cream for topping

Add the topping and maybe top with a marashino cherry.

4

Bean Soup

This recipe calls for a ham hock. That's okay if you want to make bean soup and haven't recently cooked a ham so there's a nice bone already at hand. At the Lazy Bee, whenever we cook a big roast, turkey or ham, we know that soon there's going to be soup in the refrigerator or freezer. If we're going somewhere in the RV or camping, we might can some of the soup so it can go along as a quick meal.

Large package navy beans	**Wash beans. Rinse & then soak overnight.**
Large ham hock	
8 quarts water	**Add enough water to rinse water to make eight quarts.**
2 onions, chopped fine	**Add beans and ham.**
Butter	**Boil slowly for about three hours in covered pot.**
Salt to taste	
	An hour of so before soup is ready, braise onion in butter and add to soup. Season when ready.

5

Black Rice Pudding

Forbidden Rice. I was looking for rice at Huckleberry's in Spokane to make this recipe. The name on the packet of rice brought shivers. With a name like this, the dish should be great. And, it was. Serve it hot with the topping. Add a scoop of ice cream to have an Asian "hot/cold" taste.

1 cup black rice, not wild rice	**Rinse and drain rice several times. Add**
6 cups water.	**water and bring to boil.**
1/2 cup sugar	**Reduce to a slow simmer, cover and cook**
8 ounce canned coconut milk	**45 minutes or until soft.**

Topping

Combine in a small bowl and put over each serving:

1/2 cup coconut milk

1/2 tsp. salt

2 Tbsp. sugar

Add sugar and coconut milk. Stir well and cook for 10 more minutes.

There shouldn't be any standing water. It all should be absorbed by rice and sugar mix.

Add the topping.

Blueberry Upside Down Cake

Deep into the night, a cougar was scratching the tin roof of the Lazy Bee. It was walking across the roof, looking for a way inside. Bud's son, Vince Budinger, an airline pilot who prefers sleeping on the downstairs sofa, called up to his Dad in the loft, "Dad is that you?" Bud answered, "Wasn't me." They jumped up, went to the upper deck and were shining a flashlight around when Bud said, "Might be a cougar. Their hind legs are powerful enough to get them onto this roof." If that's the case, suggested Vince, "We'd make a good meal if we continue standing where we are." They decided to come back inside and see if there was anything left of the blueberry upside down cake.

1/4 cup butter, melted

1/2 cup sugar

2 cups fresh or frozen
    blue berries

1 package yellow cake mix

Whipping cream

(Note if using frozen berries,
    don't thaw.)

Use the melted butter to coat a 9 X 13 pan.

Sprinkle with sugar and put the blueberries in the bottom.

Make the cake batter according to directions on package and spread over the blueberries.

Bake at 350 for 40-45 min. or until a toothpick comes out clean inserted in center. Serve warm with whipped cream or ice cream.

Broccoli Salad

Folks who drop by the Lazy Bee often ask for a tour. We usually begin in the dining room by saying, "Here's a sign on a board that the man who first lived here left in a closet. As you read these words, exactly as he wrote them, you'll feel how much this place meant to them, as it does to us. "This home meant more to us than you can imagine. It was a blessing from God to go threw the 3 years we lived here. It was built with great dedication. We have great memories of the joy and laughter that it brought and the Trials that made us stronger. Enjoy your stay whoever is here. Life is good only when God prevails threw everyday. Thank you, Lord God, for this place and the time we had here. " Signed Steven & Karen Ramanauskas who now live in Marble and visit us often.

1 small head cauliflower, chopped fine
5 heads broccoli, chopped fine
1 red onion, chopped fine
12 cup sunflower seeds
Whole jar bacon bits
1/2 box raisins (not kid size)
Feta cheese bits

Make a sauce of:
1 1/2 cup mayonnaise sugar to taste. Add salt and pepper to taste.

Mix sauce with the veggies, seeds, bacon bits, raising and Feta.

Broiled Fish

Guests said they were serious hikers. Bud suggested they hike to the top of Abercrombie Mountain, which is one foot short of being the tallest mountain in Northeast Washington. So Bud drove the jeep. They followed in their car and left it at Silvercreek campground. The family of four jumped into the jeep and he drove them to the Hartbauer trail head. From there they could hike to the top of the seven thousand foot mountain and come back down the other side to their car. On that hot July afternoon, they were so thrilled by the views of the alpine meadows filled with wild flowers that they called from the mountain top to share their excitement. This might be a good recipe for hikers.

2 Tbsp. chopped & toasted
   hazelnuts
2 Tbsp. ground almonds
4 oz. cheddar cheese, grated
4 Tbsp. fresh bread crumbs
1 egg
1 Tbsp. milk
4 fish fillets
2 Tbsp. flour
Salt & pepper
Cilantro springs to garnish

Preheat broiler. Put nuts in large bowl. Add cheese and bread crumbs. Mix together. In small bowl, beat egg, add milk and salt and pepper. Rinse fillets. Pat dry. Coat them in the flour, then dip into egg mixture, and then into nut mixture. Cook under broiler 5 mintues and turn once. Cook until browned.

9

Buckwheat Pancakes

The funky sofa on the upper deck is mighty comfy. Many a guest has fallen asleep there instead of in their room just a few steps away in the Tree House. Guests have spotted the futon in the outdoor, roofed and open bedroom or the one on the back deck that's near an outdoor shower and sink. They ask if that's where they can sleep. We like to sleep out-of-doors, too, especially on the futon on the back deck. It's directly under a tin roof and there's something immensely satisfying about hearing rain drops pattering overhead when you're nestled under a plump comforter. This recipe, incidentally, comes from "The Malleable Range Cookbook," printed in 1898 by that company in Indiana.

1/2 cup fine bread crumbs	**Pour milk over crumbs. Soak 30 minutes**
2 cups milk, scalded	
1/2 tsp.salt	**Add salt and the yeast cake dissolved in lukewarm water. Then**
1/4 yeast cake	**add buckwheat flour to make a batter thin**
1/2 cup lukewarm water	**enough to pour. Let rise over night. In the**
1 3/4 buckwheat flour	**morning, stir well and add molasses, 1/4 tsp.**
1 Tbsp. molasses	**soda dissolved in 1/4 cup lukewarm water, and cook on griddle.**

Cabbage Casserole

There's peace in the mountains tonight. A delicate mantle of snow covers the trees and there's two feet on the ground. Thermometer stands at minus twenty. Tractor engines will need warming in the morning. but, we won't do it like a Canadian B&B guest told us how his Grandpa did. "He brings in a can of gasoline and heats it on the wood cookstove." We gasp and ask, "Is Grandpa still with us? " He was.

1/2 cup butter

1 medium-size green cabbage,
  cored and sliced thin

1 large onion, finely chopped

1 1/2 cups milk

4 eggs, lightly beaten

15 salted crackers, finely
  crushed, about 3/4 cup

1 tsp. salt

1/8 tsp. pepper

Preheat oven to 325. Butter a two-cup casserole dish.

Melt 1/2 cup butter in large cooking pot.

Add cabbage and onion and cook over medium heat until softened, about 20 minutes. Stir in milk. Bring to boil. Lower heat to medium and simmer 5 minutes. Remove pot. Let cool. Stir in eggs. Add 1/2 cup crushed crackers, salt & pepper. Pour into prepared dish. Dust with remaining cracker crumbs. Bake at 325 for 30 min. untl heated through and top is brown.

11

Camping Casserole

Within a fifty mile radius, there are magical places of such beauty and remoteness that it takes your breath away. Views of the heaven-swept, blue skies above tiny, hidden lakes or mountain streams are so glorious they last in memory forever. We learned not to tent camp on weekends or holidays when we loaded up the gear and went to Sheep Creek, northeast of Northport. There, at our favorite spot along the creek, a long way up the mountain, others had already set up their camp. "We've been coming here over thirty years," said the woman from Spokane. When she learned we live near the Canadian border, she said, "Well, you can go home and camp outside your door." We took this casserole dish right out of there and found another place to camp along the creek. Never again. There were too many people and it was so. . .oo noisy.

2 cups meat, any kind, cut into bite-size pieces	**Mix meat, mushroom soup, water and soy sauce until smooth.**
2 cups Chinese Chow Mein noodles	
1/4 cup water	**Combine with all the other ingredients but hold out 1 cup noodles.**
1 Tbsp. soy sauce	
1 cup whole cashew nuts	
1 (4 oz) can tiny mushrooms, drained	**Mix well and place in a greased casserole dish.**
1 can mushroom soup	
1 cup celery. chopped	
1/4 cup minced onion	**Sprinkle remaining noodles on top and bake 40 minutes at 375 degrees**

Cannelloni

This is an appealing dish and worth the effort. So, put on some uplifting music and feel the passion. Pretend you're a wonderful chef. When the the kids ask why you're so excited, just say, "Tonight, we're having a wonderful surprise." When they come home from school and discover that what you've been doing wasn't baking cakes or cookies, tell them, "This morning I had a lot of hitch in my giddiup so I just had to make something Italian!

2 Tbsp. olive oil
1 1/2 cups minced onion
   (2 medium)
1 tsp. oregano
1 tsp. sugar
Salt & pepper
1/4 cup dry red wine
1 cup canned tomato sauce
1/2 cup butter
4 Tbsp. butter
1/4 cup flour (generous)
4 cups milk
1 cup parmesan cheese
3/4 tsp nutmeg
2 lb fresh spinach
1/4 lb. bacon (1/4" pieces)
4 garlic cloves, minced
1/4 cup chopped walnuts
Basic crepes

In skillet, heat 1 Tbsp. olive oil. Add cup onion and cook over medium high heat. Stir a lot until a golden color.

Add oregano and sugar and season with salt & pepper. Cook 1 min. Add the tomato sauce& wine and simmer over medium heat until slightly thick about 10 minuites.

Melt 1/2 cup butter in another pan. (Recipe continues on next page)

Continued Directions for Cannelloni

(The three components for this casserole can be assembled ahead and refrigerated until baking.)

Add 1/4 cup onion to the melted butter, cook and stir until soft, about 4 min. Whisk in the 1/4th cup of flour, and cook until well-combined. Add 2 cups milk, and then another 2 cups, whisking until smooth. Bring to boil over moderately high heat, then turn down to simmer about 2 minutes until thick. Whisk in 1/4 cup cheese, the nutmeg, pepper and 3/4 tsp. salt. Remove from heat and press a piece of plastic wrap directly on surface of this white sauce.

In another large skillet, on high heat, put in spinach by handfuls and toss until wilted. Take off stove, wipe out skillet and squeeze spinach dry, then finely chop. In the dry pan, heat remaining 1 Tbsp. olive oil. Add bacon. Cook until golden, about 3 min. Add garlic and stir another 30 sec. Add remaining 1/4 cup chopped onion and cook 3 min., till translucent. Add spinach and cook, stirring 2 min. Add the white sauce and 1 tsp. salt & pepper, Take off stove & stir in remaining 1/2 cup cheese & chopped walnuts.

Heat oven to 400. Make crepes. See recipe on page 25. Choose 16 of your best-looking crepes. Spread 3 Tbsp. spinach filing down the center of each. Roll up crepe, making neat rolled cylinders.

Spread 1/4 cup tomato sauce on bottom of 9 X 13 glass dish. Put crepes on top of sauce. Spread remaining white sauce over. Top with 1/4 cup cheese. Bake 25 min. or until crepes are heated through. Let stand a few minutes before serving.

Cheese and Corn Chowder

There something more substantial when you think of a chowder. It's not a soup. That's more of a liquid base, or a stew that has more chunky ingredients in it. A chowder takes the middle ground. The recipe for this one comes out just as tasty made with fresh corn as it does with canned.

1/4 cup butter	Melt butter in pan over low heat.
1/4 cup chopped onion	Add onion and cook until transparent, not brown.
1/4 cup flour	Add flour & blend
4 cups milk	thoroughly.
2 cans creamed corn	Add milk slowly and stir until smooth and thickened.
2 cups shredded cheese	Stir in corn and cheese.
2 tsp. salt	Heat until cheese melts. Don't boil. Add seasonings. Makes 6-8 servings.
1/4 tsp. pepper	

Cheese Ball

People who live in the woods burn a lot of forest debris, piles and piles of downed branches, twigs, underbrush, and dead trees. Collecting this into piles that we call slash is an exercise like doing yoga, a little more brisk but the same stretching, tugging, bending and exercising of muscles. After burning a pile or two, you'll return to the house with rosy cheeks and a sense of accomplishment. The task may seem a challenge at first, especially if the pile is wet. To get a fire going in wet debris, and keep it going, is an acquired art, much like making this large cheese ball.

8 ounces cream cheese, softened

8 ounces port wine cheese food

3 cups sharp cheddar cheese
   softened

1 cup sliced almonds or pecans
   toasted

1/4 cup pimento, chopped

1/2 cup green pepper, chopped

2 Tbsp. onion, finely chopped

1 tsp. Worchestershire sauce

Mix the cheeses and stir until combined. Add the rest of ingredients, except the nuts.

Spoon into center square of plastic food wrap. Using your hands, gently mold into ball and wrap in plastic.

Refrigerate at least 1 hour.

Roll in the toasted almonds or coarsely chopped pecans.

Serve with raw veggies or crackers.

Cheese Bread

Junk in the thrift store was piled high. Bud was lost amongst the overflowing rows, looking for a book or tractor part. I waited for him at the check out counter and spied an unusual cookbook laying in the only cleared space in the store. On the cover was a glossy picture of a small, rustic Kentucky cabin. I picked it up. The recipes called for squirrel or whiskey or other ingredients foreign to my cupboard. Inside the book were photos of the cabin's interior and a wood cook stove. "This for sale?" I asked. The lady behind the counter said, "Only thing in this store that isn't." I got to thinking. There are so many cookbooks. Why does one appeal and another does not? Perhaps this story brought a smile. Does this recipe do that for you?

2 Tbsp. butter	Heat broiler.
3 Tbsp. olive oil	In small saucepan, cook butter 1 min. until it is melted. Remove from heat and stir in the oil. cheese and garlic.
1/2 cup Parmesan cheese	
6 cloves garlic, peeled and chopped	
1 loaf Italian bread, halved lengthwise	Spread mixture over the halved pieces of bread. Broil 5 min. or until crisp and light brown.

Cherry Angel Torte

A physican, on a fellowship in Seattle, was taking his parents, his wife's parents and their two young children on a whirlwind tour of the Pacific Northwest before they all returned to the Netherlands. "Your e-mail made the Lazy Bee sound so wonderful that we wanted to stay two nights. We have a mountain in our country, too. It's in the North where we live and it's thirty-six feet tall. There are many folk tales about a witch who lives there." Here's a dish that looks like a mountain. We served it for them as a Western 'comfort meal' after the pot roast.

1 prepared Angel Food Cake

8 ounce cream cheese,
   softened

1 cup sugar

1 cup confectioners' sugar

1 carton 16 ounce frozen
   whipped topping, thawed

1 large can cherry or
   blueberry pie filling

Beat cream cheese and and sugars until smooth.

Fold in whipped topping.

Split cake into four horizontal layers.

Place bottom layer on a serving plate. Top with one-fourth of the whipped mixture and a fourth of the pie filling.

Repeat three more layers.

Refrigerate until serving.
12-16 servings

Chipped Corn Beef Casserole

If you like to soak in mineral hot springs, just across the border into British Columbia, there are several a few hours away. Ainsworth is the closest. It has a cave as well as large and small pools, plus a bitter cold one. The waters in the cave come from a steamy shower of mineralized water that falls from the roof to form a waist-deep natural steam bath. At Halcayon Hot Springs further on up into Canada, there is the softest imaginable water with not a hint of sulfur. Chalets at Halcayon are new. It's a romatic get-away with creature comforts that include furnished kitchens and barbeque gas grills. No grocery stores are anywhere near, so you must bring your own food. Coffee and tea is on the counter. Maybe you can bring this casserole and reheat it in the microwave.

1 package macroni & cheese	**Prepare the macroni & cheese according to the**
1 can mushroom soup	**directions on package.**
1 cup milk	**Mix with soup, milk, onion, cheese and dried**
Minced onion to taste	**corned beef.**
1 cup shredded sharp cheddar utes cheese	**Bake covered 30 min- at 350 degrees.**
2 three-ounce jars of corned beef dried, chopped	

Cookie Monster Oatmeal Cookies

A Cookie Monster was at the Lazy Bee. Son-in-law Brady Berry likes to get up in the middle of the night to find cookies. He's not the only one. Others now follow his example. A delegation of two adults and four children once trudged into the kitchen to find me. Marty Budinger gripped my shoulders and looked me in the eye. "No fair. Give us a clue." I suggested that they look on the third shelf in the barn freezer. Behind three large bags of shredded cheese, they'd find these oatmeal cookies. "These cookies would even be better if you'd add chocolate chips," said Bud.

Preheat oven to 350

1 cup granulated sugar
1 cup vegetable shortening

Grease cookie sheets

Beat shortening and

sugars until creamy.

2 eggs
2 tsp. vanilla
2 Tbsp. milk
2 cups flour
1 tsp. baking power

Add eggs, vanilla and
and milk. Mix well.

1 tsp. baking soda
1 tsp. salt
2 cups old-fashioned
   oatmeal
1 cup raisins or
   combo of coconut, or
   chopped nuts

Combine flour, baking
poweder, soda, salt.

Add to shortening mix
then add additions
and bake 10 minutes
until brown

20

Corn Casserole

Six stray cats showed up here last year. The first was a black mama and her two wild kittens. "Are you feeding them?" asked Bud. A few months later, after they'd gobbled up big sacks of food, the father, a huge, yellow guy came and ate up all their food. BZ Israel, a neighbor, took the mama to add to his stock of cats that patrol his organic farm for gophers. The dad and teenage cats got a long ride up a mountain. When another good-looking cat arrived, Gay Miller liked him so she whisked him home. The last to arrive is a stripped, brown cat who moves around the grounds like a prince on tall, skinny, ski-pole legs. He gets close enough to let us know he likes our leftovers.

1 stick butter
1 large onion, chopped
1 green pepper, chopped
2 eggs, slightly beaten
1 15 ounce can creamed corn
    drained
1 15 ounce whole kernel
    corn and liquid
1 box Jiffy corn muffin mix
1/2 tsp. salt
1/4 tsp. garlic powder
1 cup sour cream
1 cup cheddar cheese, grated

Heat oven to 400.

Saute onion and green pepper in butter.

Add eggs, both cans corn & liquid, Jiffy mix, salt, sour cream and cheddar cheese. Pour into 9 s 13 pan and bake 45 min. or until golden brown. Last 5 min. top with extra cheese.

Corned Beef

Early one chilly November morning, the sun was just coming up when Bud stopped the jeep on a mountainside. We were sipping hot coffee from a thermos when through the rising mist we saw a majestic herd of elk. The huge bull led a long line of smaller cows. He was gorgeous. Later when elk were in season, Vince Budinger came to the Lazy Bee so he and his Dad could hatch a plan to snare one. The elk must have heard about their elaborate game plan. They were no where to be found on Wild Rose Ridge where we'd seen them. You won't find that place on a map. It's a name we gave the clear-cut because of its many wild rose bushes.

4 lb. corned beef brisket	Cover brisket with 1/2 inch of water in roasting pan.
12 ounces of beer	Add beer, onions, celery.
1 small onion, peeled & quartered	Cover and place in 250-300 degree oven for 4 1/2 hr.
2 whole stalks celery wtih leaves	
6-8 potatoes, peeled & halved	Remove pan. Discard onions and celery. Add potatoes, carrots and
1 lb. carrots, peeled & halved	cabbage and cook 1 hr. longer, adding more water if needed.
Medium head green cabbage, quartered	
	Cook a little longer if vegetables aren't fork ready.

Country Fried Steak

Sam and Karla Nigh, bed and breakfast guests from California, said the Lazy Bee was their kind of a place. They stayed here while visiting her sister, Terri, and husband, who live a few miles up the road off Cedar Creek. Appealing to the Nighs, in addition to the following recipe, is the close rapport we have with our neighbors. They also like our simpler life style and our many freedoms now lost to them in a big city. "In some cities in California, houses are twelve feet from each other," said Karla. "They cost a fortune and are built on so little land. None of them could have a shooting range or large bouche ball court in the yard."

Box prepared country gravy

Beat eggs and add buttermilk.

1 cup buttermilk

Dip steaks into the egg mixture.

2 eggs

Then, into the seasoned flour.

2 cups flour, seasoned,
    1 tsp. salt
    1 tsp. pepper
    1/2 tsp. rosemary
    1/2 tsp. sage
    1 tsp. Dash

Again, into the liquid batter.

Once again into the flour mix.

Fry steak individually in oil.
Keep warm while making
gravy of pan juices and milk
and a little salt to taste.

Cube Steaks

23

Crab and Shrimp Dip

My friend Judge Kathleen O'Connor says there are few original recipes. This one I got from Ellen Dilly who received a copy from Jean Edgerton who got it from Virginia Whitehouse who got it from a friend in Hawaii. Good ones must have a travel history. It's served with crackers and is finger-licking good, no matter who originiated it.

1 1/2 cup imitation crab

1 1/2 cup fresh shrimp (the tiny ones)

1 cup mayonnaise

1 cup Cheddar cheese, grated

3/4 cup diced onions

Salt and pepper

Put crab and shrimp in a bowl and smash with a fork.

Add other ingredients and mix well.

Bake uncovered in a glass dish at 350 for 15 minutes.

Serve hot with crackers.

Crepes

A light, thin crepe is so versatile. Use it for lunch or breakfast. Roll it up with a meat, or a vegetable like asparagus, and serve a sauce over it. Better yet, serve it for breakfast with condiments of applesauce, whipped cream and huckleberry sauce.

2 eggs

2/3 cup milk

1 Tbsp. butter or margarine, melted

1/2 cup unsifted flour

1/4 tsp. salt

In medium bowl, beat eggs thoroughly.

Beat in flour and salt until batter is smooth.

Coat a small skillet or crepe pan with salad oil. Then heat over medium heat until hot but not so hot that it smokes.

Cook each crepe about two minutes on the first side, then flip and brown quickly on the other side.

Remove from skillet and keep warm on a cookie sheet in an oven about 250 degrees.

Crispy Critters

The world floats by. Joy dances in. A cool breeze sways the hammock. Your eyes feast upon tops of tall trees waving in the wind. Isn't it glorious just being here in the NOW, not worrying about tomorrow's problems or yesterday's sorrows? Just being. Truly seeing the pale blueness of the sky or the clouds moving so slowly. A thought rushes in. Can it be a desire to make these simple Crispy Critters? Another time, perhaps. Just living in the present is so delicious. So stop. Let joy in. "But, If you do make these sweet and salty cookies," says Karen Lair of Florida, "Watch out, they can be addictive."

1 package (2 cups) Nestle Morsels, regular milk chocolate or peanut butter or a mix of both	Microwave morsels 30-40 seconds until smooth.
	Whip until unchunky.
1 cup dry roasted peanuts or pretzels (chopped)	Stir together.
1 cup Chinese noodles	
	Drop off by teaspoons onto cookie sheet and Bag and refrigerate.

Crockpot Favorite

We applied and received a FLEP financial aid grant to reduce the fuel load in our forest. For years, we and the neighboring children carted off limbs from cut-up downed trees, cleared areas of underbrush, raked and burned the slash. No matter how much work we did, the forest marched ahead, unrelenting in its need for help against mistletoe, pine beatles and root rot. Now, we were able to hire the professional services of Silvertip Forestry, so I'd be out of the house doing this physically-demanding work for two or more weeks. I needed hearty crockpot recipes so a meal would be ready when we came in for lunch. This recipe Gay gave me turned out to be one of the best. It makes enough to serve six or more, with enough left over for another meal.

4-6 boneless chicken breasts

2 packages Stovetop dressing

Dried cranberries (lots)

Layer of shredded cheese

**2 cans mushroom soup, or
1 can water and 1 can soup**

2 cans water

Sage and salt to taste

**Grease a large crockpot.
Make 2 layers of chicken,
with a handfull of the dried
cranberries, cheese and
seasonings.**

**Pour liquid over the top,
finishing with the cheese.**

**Turn crockpot to low.
Cook 6 to 8 hours. Watch
to be sure there's enough
liquid, adding more
if necessary. Add veggies
and a salad to complete
the meal.**

Crunchy Peanut Butter Cookies

We like to use white, embroidered pillowcases at the Lazy Bee for guest beds. Many a treasure has been found in Midwest or Texas antique stores. They are made of the softest cotton and are a joy to handle. I love laundering and ironing them, using a delicate linen spray. As I place a set on a freshly-made up bed, I wonder whose hands have made these lovely cases. Is anyone making these cookies?

9 Tbsp. butter
1/2 cup chunky peanut butter
1 1/2 cup sugar
1 egg, lightly beaten
1 cup flour
1/2 tsp. baking powder
Pinch of salt
1/2 cup unsalted peanuts.
   chopped

Preheat oven to 375
Grease 2 baking sheets
with butter.

In a large bowl, beat
butter & peanut butter
together. Gradually
add sugar and beat
together well.

Add beaten egg, a little
at a time. Stir in flour,
baking powder and salt
Add peanuts and make
soft dough. Wrap in
plastic wrap & chill 30
min. Make 20 balls &
place 2 inches apart.
Flatten with your hand.
Bake 15 minutes.

Crusty Baked Apples

The CJ5 Jeep, with twelve gears, has made countless trips up the beckoning mountains. It chugs across ruts on trails, bumps over downed trees and goes over tall mounds. You must step high to get into it. If you're a little boy, you leap into the back seat. Maybe you'll stand up, hold onto the tall, metal rollbar and feel like King of the World. Little girls like to wrap up in a big blanket. We all like peering over the edge of the mountain. How far up we are! Apples in this recipe should be crowded together just like people sometimes are in the jeep. Put them in a greased baking pan and nestle them close so the topping doesn't slide off.

6 tart apples, cored and top peeled at the top	Put cored apples into a baking dish, pared side up.
6 Tbsp. butter	
6 Tbsp. flour	Melt butter and stir in the flour, mixing well.
1 1/2 cups brown sugar	Add brown sugar and vanilla. Spread mixture on top of the apples.
1 1/2 tsp. vanilla.	
	Bake in 425 degree oven until crust sets, about 10 to 15 minutes.
	Lower to 350 degrees and bake another 40-45 min, about 1 hr. baking time.

29

Dandelion Salad

Young dandelion leaves make a tasty salad if mixed with other greens. Use the youngest leaves from plants. They're the best. Look for plants that aren't near dusty or heavily traveled places in your yard, the neighbor's backyard, or the vacant lot down the way. Don't look for them in a grocery store until this recipe takes off and more people find out how tasty dandelion leaves can be in a salad.

Dandelion leaves, enough to make 2 cups	**Wash & dry dandelion leaves and other greens**
Assorted salad greens, 4 to 5 cups	**Set aside in big pieces in a serving bowl.**
6 slices bacon, cut into pieces	**Heat bacon strips in a pan until fat melts and bacon get crisp.**
2 Tbsp. red wine vinegar	**Stir vinegar into the fat and pour the whole lot over salad greens and serve at once.**

Decadent French Toast

Fran and Carl Ogren live in the Northport area on a remote ranch. As sustainable farmers, they use a wood cook stove and solar panels for their freezers. Carl cuts the hay they raise to feed their livestock with a hand sythe. They buy only a few items, like salt. We had a memorable dinner there once: butter she'd churned, trout he'd caught, pie from the huckleberries they'd picked. There's a wood cookstove in the Lazy Bee kitchen just like Fran's where this dish might be in the range baking for breakfast.

1 Tbsp. corn syrup
1/2 cup brown sugar, firmly packed
3 Tbsp. butter
16 slices wheat sandwich bread
5 eggs
1 1/2 cups milk
1 tsp. vanilla

Topping

1 1/2 cup fresh berries or package frozen

1/2 cup sour cream

Combine brown sugar, corn syrup and butter in saucepan and heat & stir until bubbly. Pour into a 9 X 13 pan.

Nestle 2 layers of bread slices in the pan. Mix eggs, milk and vanilla & pour over bread. Cover. Refrigerate over night. Next day, put uncovered pan in preheated 350 oven for 45 minutes. Use spatula to take out of pan making sure carmelized portion is on the top.

31

Different Cobbler

Foreign Film Nights at the Community College in Colville are mini-courses in art, history or culture. Professors from Washington State University who are either from the same country as the film, or whose specialty is that country, introduce the film and lead the audience discussions afterwards. I wish I'd been there the night my favorite film, Antonnia's Line, was shown. The free film series is held in October but that night I was at the Lazy Bee serving this cobbler to guests.

2 quarts strawberries,
  hulled & halved
2/3 cup sugar
1/4 cup orange juice
2 Tbsp. quick tapioca
1/2 tsp. cinnamon

Topping:
1 cup flour
5 Tbsp. sugar
1/4 tsp. baking soda
14 tsp. salt
6 Tbsp. milk
3 Tbsp. sour cream
3 Tbsp. butter

Heat oven to 350.
In large bowl, mix together strawberries, sugar, orange juice, cinnamon & nutmeg. Spoon into 6 cup baking dish.

In medium bowl, whisk together flour, sugar, salt and baking soda. Stir in milk, sour cream and the butter until smooth. Dollop this over fruit. Put l Tbsp. sugar over. Bake at 350 for 35-40 minutes utnil bubbly & browned. Serve warm.

Different Lemon Cake

Neighbor Dawn Owings, mother of four, was on vacation. from her job at the clinic. "The first day I was up early as ever. I washed all the windows that day. By the third day, I was sleeping later." Dawn collects cookbooks and told me she bought the first version of this cookbook at the local Goodwill for $1.99. Now that's a big compliment because it was priced higher than most of their books. I learned all this because Dawn called to ask the size of a pan for this desert on the fourth day of her vacation. Recipes in this edition have been edited by her discerning eye. In case I forget, use a 9 X 13 pan.

1 package lemon cake mix	Heat oven to 350. Grease glass pan and dust with flour.
1 package lemon jello	
3/4 cup water	Make cake according to directions on box and add jello.
3/4 cup oil	
4 eggs well beaten	While cake is baking, mix juice and grated rind of lemons with powdered sugar.
2 lemons	
2 cups powdered sugar	
	Bake 35 to 40 minutes. When cake is done, prick with a fork and spread juice mixture over hot cake.

Dorothea's Chocolate Chip Cookies

Panic. This recipe was lost. Dorothea's called for blended oatmeal. That means in a blender to a fine powder. Nothing with blended oatmeal could be found in cookbooks or the Internet. What to do? When was it last used? Ah ha! Didn't we take a copy in the RV for Jennifer Hamilton who lives in San Miguel d'Alende, the time we drove the RV all the way into central Mexico? So finding a beloved but lost recipe is boon to the soul. Obviously it *was* in the RV.

Preheat oven to 325 degrees   **Grease cookie sheets**

2 cups real butter   **Cream butter and both**
2 cups sugar   **sugars. Add eggs**
2 cups brown sugar   **and vanilla.**

2 eggs
2 tsp. vanilla
2 1/2 cups flour   **Mix together with**
1 1/2 cups blended oatmeal   **oatmeal, salt, baking**
1/2 cup old-fashioned   **powder and soda.**
oatmeal
2 tsp. soda   **Add chocolate chips,**
l tsp. salt   **candy, nuts and roll**
2 tsp. baking powder   **tight into balls and**
    place two inches
    apart on lightly greased
1 8oz. Hershey bar, grated   **cookie sheets.**
24 oz. chocolate chips
3 cup chopped nuts   **Bake 10-12 minutes.**
    Makes 112 cookies.

34

Dressed-up Green Salad

A young man came West from Detroit to hike Abercrombie Mountain. He fell in love with the area and bought eight acres. He returned with his bride, a city gal he wooed beneath her window wearing a white cape and carrying a red rose in his teeth. His vision and beginning carpentry skills created this two-story cabin with lumber from the forest and items he scavanged wherever he could find them. Today, Steve Ramanauskas is a highly-regarded builder. His wife, Karen, is an expert stained glass designer. We asked her to make a large stained glass scene of mountains for the livingroom. Karen might create salads like this.

6 cups salad greens
2 medium navel oranges
1 cup halved red grapes
1/2 cup golden raisins
1/4 cup chopped red onion
1/4 cup sliced almonds
4 pieces bacon, cooked and
    crumbled

DRESSING:
1/2 cup mayonnaise
1/2 cup honey
1/4 cup orange juice
2 Tbsp. grated orange peel

In a large salad bowl, combine the first seven ingredients.

In a bowl, whisk together mayonnaise, honey, orange juice and peel.

Serve the dressing with the salad. Refrigerate leftovers.

(6 servings & 1 cup dressing)

35

Enchilada Casserole

"Where can you have so much fun for five dollars?" asked a man who was unloading his truck at the Kettle Falls landfill. He was obviously enjoying what for him was an adventure. For me, going to the landfill is a challenge. A woman attendant there has suggested that I not come back until I learn to back up a trailer. "Our summer help will be gone soon and there will be no one who can do it for you," she said. Although backing a trailer is not in my skill bank, this casserole is one that never fails. It's quick and easy.

Left-over cooked chicken	**Cut corn torillas in strips**
Large can Enchilada Sauce	**Place cut-up chicken pieces in greased casserole dish**
Package corn Tortillas	**Top with layer of tortills, cheese and oilves**
Can black oilves, drained	**Make another layer of chicken, tortillas, and olives.**
Package shredded cheese	**Cover with enchalida sauce**
Sour Cream topping	**Bake 350 degrees 30min.**
	Top with sour cream

Filet of Beef

Wild turkeys do fly. High, enough to roost in the tall fir and larch trees at the Lazy Bee. A lone male stayed behind one day. Early morning, he started yelling from the tree-top. Turkeys were in season. Bud called down from the office, "We're having turkey for dinner. I'm busy in the office so I'll collect it later.." When he went to pick up the bird, it was gone. Was it taken by a bigger animal? Had his companion come for him?

4-5 lb rib-eye roast
4 cloves garlic, cut in slivers
1 cup Dijon mustard
1/4 cup soy sauce
4 Tbsp. coarsely ground
   pepper

Sauce
1/4 cup Dijon mustard
1 Tbsp. soy sauce
1 cup beef stock
1 Tbsp. pepper

Whisk sauce ingredients together, then heat through. Serve sauce with roast.

Insert garlic slivers into incisions cut at intervals in meat in roasting pan.

Combine mustard and soy sauce and spread over roast. Top with pepper. Let roast sit at room temp. up to 3 hr.

Preheat oven to 350. Insert thermometer in center of roast. Cook until it reads 120 for rare, about 1 1/2 hr. Remove from oven and let sit on cutting board for 15 minutes. Carve.

Fish Batter

On the Columbia River, Black Sand Beach is downstream from the store at the Waneta Border. To get there, drive about 3/4 mile midway up a hill, take a sharp left and go over the Railroad tracks. The road after the tracks is deeply rutted, almost impassable. Park in the woods above the river and walk down to the glittering sand beach. If you make it, you'll probably find Kathleen Johnson, one of the area's most dedicated fishermen. She often stays until the sun goes down and might use this batter for her freshly caught trout.

2 cups flour	**Combine ingredients.**
3 cups pancake mix	**Dip moist fish pieces lightly in flour.**
3 cups club soda	
1 Tbsp. onion powder	**Dust off any excess flour and let fish pieces dry on waxed paper about five minutes.**
1 Tbsp. seasoned salt	**Whip pancake mix with club soda, not too thick or thin. Beat in onion powder & salt. Dip the the pieces into batter & cook in hot oil about 4 minutes each side.**

Five Star Devilded Eggs

Thanksgiving feasts at the Lazy Bee once were served on a long, narrow table made of pine wood which almost ran the entire length of the downstairs. Heaped before the twenty or so guests would be many platters of traditional foods. Then Alice would arrive with her crew and a gigantic plate of deviled eggs as a side dish. "With so much food here, how can we eat all these eggs?" At the end of the whopping meal, not one deviled egg remained. Alice shares some tips that make them so appetizing.

6 eggs

2-3 Tbsp. Mayonnaise

1 tsp. honey mustard

1 tsp. pickle juice

Salt & pepper to taste

Paprika

Cover eggs with cold water. heating slowly to simmering. Cook 20 to 25 minutes. Don't boil. Run cold water over the eggs and leave until cold.

Shell eggs and cut into halves lengthwise.

Remove yolks.

Combine yolks, mustard, pickle juice & seasonings with the yolks. Beat until smooth and creamy with an electric mixer.

Spoon mixture into egg halves and sprinkle with paprika.

Five Star Coleslaw

Here's a delightful version of coleslaw from Judy Martin. She calls it Tropical Coleslaw, perhaps because of the unique ingredients are so colorful. In my collection, it gets five stars or top billing. If you're clumsy chopping ingredients, ask someone else to hold the cabbage while you chop. You'll save your fingers. This holds a few days refrigerated. If there are any leftovers.

3 cups cabbage, shredded

Combine ingredients.

2 ribs celery, chopped

Add more yogurt or else sour cream with a bit

1 can pinapple tidbits

of sugar if needed.

1/2 golden raisins

You can use sour cream with a little sugar instead

1 banana, chopped

of the yogurt.

1/2 cup walnuts, coarsely chopped
1/2 tsp. salt

This fills a big bowl.

l can mandarin oranges, drained

1/2 cup shredded coconut
1 carton lemon yogurt, 8 oz.

40

Ginger Chicken

Rural America has women with exceptional talents. Women in a local group were asked to tell about their skills. One said, "I've been president of every group to which I've belonged. I like to make presentations." Another said she has a full-time professional career, and among her other skills, is potter, gardener, community organizer. A five-month expectant flight attendant said, "In January when the baby comes, I'll have more time to do things for this group."When the spontaneous laughter died down, I thought about my talent. Perhaps it is finding fabulous chicken recipes like this.

4 Tbsp. chopped gingerroot, (fresh) divided

5 cloves garlic, peeled and minced.

1 tsp. salt

1/2 tsp. pepper

Heat oven 400 degrees

In bowl, combine 3 Tbsp. gingerroot, garlic, salt , pepper. Spread half in side cavity and the rest under the loosened skin.

l roasting chicken, about 6 lb.

1 orange, zested and juiced rind reserved

2 Tbsp. soy sauce

Put orange rind inside cavity. Roast 20 min. Reduce to 350 and roast l hr. more. In skillet, put 1/2 cup juice, soy sauce & rest of ginger to boil. Cook 3 minutes. Stir in l Tbsp.zest. Brush over chicken last 30 min.

Glazed Ham Slices

Big Foot was sighted a few miles north of the Lazy Bee. In the mid 1980's, a frightened young bride warned her husband in the middle of winter, "Don't go outside tonight. Something horrible is out there." When they ventured out in the morning, they took photos of huge human-like footprints in the snow. Recently, in the summertime, in that same area, people said they smelled a terrible stench like burned hair in the air several nights. Nearby Indian tribes, the Spokanes, Colvilles, Yakamas, all tell similar tales. This story is not told here to frighten you from trying this recipe.

4 thick ham slices

4 Tbsp. brown sugar

2 Tsp mustard powder

4 Tbsp. butter

8 slices pineapple

In a big skillet, heat the ham slices, two at a time.

Combine brown sugar and mustard in a dish. Melt butter in another skillet. Add the slices of pineapple and cook 2 minutes to heat, turning once. Sprinkle with sugar mixture and cook over lot heat until sugar is melted and pineapple glazes on both sides.

Green Beans in the Crockpot

Menu planning is necessary if six or more guests are going to be staying longer than one night. If an item is needed for a dish, and hasn't been obtained ahead of time, we can't slip off to the store to get it. Canada is closer but currently we can't bring any meat products, eggs, citrus, or plants across the border Not even cat food due to the little bit of meat in it. For large groups, the crockpot comes in handy. Green beans in a crockpot will leave room for other dishes being prepared on the stove.

8 cups green beans

1 cup chopped onions

1/2 cup chopped green peppers

Small can mushrooms

4 Tbsp. brown sugar

6 Tbsp. butter

Pepper

Combine beans, onions, mushrooms and peppers in the crockpot.

Sprinkle with brown sugar, dot with butter and sprinkle with a little bit of pepper.

Cover and cook on high three hours. Stir before serving.

Hamburger Hot Dish

Mountain folks have technology just like city folks, but in different forms. Internet is the slow-paced dial-up, but some of the more proficient users around here get it faster via satillite. Mail comes. Residents talk about Bill, our post-man, as if he's a neighbor. Same goes for Shane, our UPS delivery guy. When he drives down the driveway in his brown truck, he takes time to chat. They're both happy guys who love their jobs. Catalogs and the Internet put the world at our door. It's a bit expensive if Bud is shopping. Here's a casserole he likes to make.

1 lb. hamburger 1 1/2 cup onions 1 can tomato soup	Saute onions in large skillet. Brown the hamburger in same pan.
1 eight-ounce can tomato sauce and 2 crushed garlic buds. Small package egg noodles	Add tomato soup, tomato sauce, garlic, salt & pepper. Cook on low heat 10 min.
1 3-ounce pkg. cream cheese, soft	In separate pan, cook. and drain noodles. Add, them to the hamburger.
1 cup Cheddar cheese	Add cream cheese, sour cream and cheddar
1 cup sour cream	cheese and heat thru.

44

Heaven Under the Stars

It's heaven to sleep under the stars, the night sky ablaze with their secrets. Usually we sleep with a tent overhead. But once we forgot the main tent. Only the rain fly and poles made it. Bud, being the creative engineer he is, rigged a canopy. We were at Trout Lake, west of Kettle Falls in Sherman Pass. The sites at the tucked-away forest service camp are unique. One even has a little bridge leading to it. "Just hope it doesn't rain and that there aren't too many mosquitos," said Bud. All alone on the mountaintop that warm August night, we heated this pre-baked casserole over a campfire.

4 large potatoes, quartered	**Heat oven to 350.**
2 stalks celery, sliced	**Grease 2-quart dish.**
2 carrots, sliced	**Combine potatoes, celery, carrots and onion**
1 onion, chopped	**and place in dish. Over top, crumble the ground**
1 lb. lean ground beef	**beef.**
1 can tomato soup, thinned	**Pour soup over the top.**
	Bake uncovered for two hours or until meat is browned.

Holiday Dessert

Mountains can be tough survival schools, pushing the folks who live in them to grow in ways they might have if they lived in the city. Bud learns to repair tractors. I build a chimney and walkways with stones that I carry away from Lott's hill in the jeep. When Dawn Owings tells me about her new medical career, she also tells about one of her favorite recipes handed down from her New York Jewish nurse grandmother. "I remember seeing it amongst all the other desserts around the holidays. Michael, Matthew, Kaylah and Dillon, my children, ask for it now as well."

1 large package cranberry jello (or orange or any red type)	Make jello according to package directions.
16 ounce container sour cream	Refrigerate and when the jello is starting to jell,
1 can whole berry cranberry sauce	mix in the sour cream and the cranberry sauce.
	Pour into a bowl or a jello mold.

Household Hints

The unstructured kitchen gives the feeling of an old-fashioned kitchen that just "growed." Many country kitchens fit this description. The countrified atmosphere keeps everything in view: a natural jumble of beloved jars, baskets, glasses, exposed pots and pans, open shelving that shows the way food is cooked. Having much-used dishes and equipment close at hand saves time, just like a few household hints like these.

Wrap celery in foil.

In the refrigerator, it ought to last for weeks.

Clean a thermos bottle.

Fill bottle with water, drop in four Alka Seltzer tablets. Let soak for an hour or so.

Unclog a drain.

Drop 3 Alka Seltzer tablets down the drain, followed by one cup of white vinegar. Wait a few minutes & run the hot water.

Leftover wine (what's that?)

Freeze in ice cube trays for use in casseroles or sauces.

A sealed envelope

Put it in the freezer a few hours. Then slide a knife under the flap. It's easy to open.

Lasagna on Top Stove

Take a large nonstick skillet that has a lid and a few ingredients can make a unique lasagna on top the stove. I use a three-inch tall cast iron pot and it also works, too. You add the ingredients in steps that build until a layered lagasna appears as if by magic. But, the order of when to add what is critical. It serves at least 10 to 12.

1 28-oz. can diced tomatoes
1 Tbsp. olive oil
1 medium onion, minced
Salt & pepper
3 cloves garlic, minced
1/8 tsp. red pepper flakes
1 pound hamburger
10 curly-edged pieces of
   lasagna, broken into
   two-inch pieces
1 8-ounce can tomato sauce
1/2 cup plus 2 Tbsp.
   grated Parmesan cheese
1 cup ricotta cheese
     chopped

(Sprinkle with 3 Tbsp. fresh,
   chopped cilantro.)

Saute the onion, garlic and meat in the skillet.

Scatter the broken lasagna noodles over the meat but do not stir.

Pour diced tomatoes and tomato sauce over the noodles and bring to simmer, reduce to low, cover and simmer, stirring occasionally for 20 minutes.
Remove skillet from stove & stir the Parmesan cheese and let it soften off heat. Season with salt & Dot with heaping tsp. ricotta & let stand 5 min.

Layered Pineapple Salad

The first pair of swallows came to the Lazy Bee and built their nest in a loose board above our back deck. One morning they were making a terrible ruckus. I rushed out the door and saw a squirrel climbing down the siding with a baby swallow in its mouth. The parents were wild, darting every which way. I yelled, "Bud, a squirrel is killing baby birds." He rushed down from the office with a rifle and shot the squirrel. It lay on the ground, the parents pecking away at it. A couple of weeks went by. The parents must have waited until we both were in the barnyard. They flew around us in three low circles before heading south with with their two young ones. We cheer the arrival of their many descendants each May because our mosquito patrol has arrived. See them high in the sky, darting and gracefully swooping. This salad is worth a cheer or two, too!

2 packages lemon jello
3 cups hot water
1 lb. can crushed pineapple, drained
12 marshmellows, cut fine
3 bananas, cut fine
1 cup pineapple juice
1 egg or yolk beaten well
1 1/2 Tbsp. flour
1/2 cup sugar
1/2 pint whipping cream
1 cup grated Cheddar cheese

Prepare jello in 3 cup hot water. Cool.

Add pineapple, marsh-mellows and bananas. Chill in large, flat pan.

Heat pineapple juice. Add beaten egg yolk, flour & sugar. Cook till thick. Fold in whipped cream. Spread on top with grated cheese.

49

Lemon Chicken

Mud season: gray days, soggy, rutted roads and driveways. Cold, rainy days. Bread dough won't rise. Vehicles get stuck in deep ruts. Mud is tracked into the house. But, one good thing does take place between March and May. The wood stove is used every day. Perhaps, it's to make oatmeal, heat soup for lunch, or cook a chicken in the oven.

4 to 6 lb. chicken at
    room temperature

1 lemon

1 Tbsp. sea salt

1 large Tbsp. butter

Olive oil

Preheat oven to 425.

Put chicken in roasting pan, one half of lemon in the cavity with a bit of salt.

Rub butter over skin.

Dribble a little oil over it, too. Cook 1 hr. and 15 minutes.

Take out of oven and let sit 15 min., sprinkling remaining salt and squeezing the last 1/2 lemon juices over it.

Slice and serve.

Lemon Curd - Clotted Cream

It would have more correct if we had called the teas we gave one summer, "Afternoon Tea" rather than "High Tea." In England, High Tea is served at six o'clock and has more substantial fare and meat. In Canada, Devonshire Cream or clotted cream, can be found at some super markets. We presented guests with five different "savories" or delicately cut-up sandwiches with varied toppings, an interlude of huge raspberries filled with chocolate chips and bowls of whipped cream. This was followed by scones and Lemon Curd and Clotted Cream. We ended with five sweets. Two types of tea were poured: stronger for the sandwiches, herbal for the sweets. Sandy Everson let us borrow her great-grandmother's Victorian cups and saucers and three Dione quintuplet spoons, each shaped like a child.

Lemon Curd:

In top of double boiler, put peel, juice, eggs, butter & sugar over simmering water. Stir until sugar disolves. Stir until smooth and thickened. Put in quart jar in refrigerator Use within 2 weeks.

Juice of four lemons

Four eggs, beaten

1/2 cup butter in pieces

2 cups sugar

Clotted Cream:
Beat 1 cup whipping cream. Whisk in 1/3 cup sour cream and 1 Tbsp. Confectioners Sugar.

Peel of lemons, grated

51

Memorable Zucchini Bread

We were invited to Ken Philipps farm on Spanish Prairie Road west of Colville. "You enter a country home through the kitchen," he said. "Come in and meet the wife." As we entered, there was the heavenly and unmistakable scent of zucchini bread just out of the oven. Marge was in the living room and said indeed she'd just taken some zucchini bread out of the oven. After chatting with her awhile, we went outside with Ken to see an area along the creek he'd been telling us about, a place where Indians once camped. Before we left, Marge came out and gave us a loaf of this most incredible tasting bread. It's a five-star recipe for sure and makes a large panful or five small loaves.

1 cup raisins
1/4 cup water
1/2 cup shortening
2 cup sugar
2 eggs
1 tsp. vanilla
3 3/4 cup grated, unpeeled
   raw zucchini
1 tsp. grated orange peel
2 cups sifted flour
2 tsp. soda
1 tsp. cinnamon
1/2 tsp. salt
1 cup chopped nuts
Powdered sugar

In small saucepan, combine raisins and water; bring to a boil. Remove from heat and cool. Cream shortening and sugar until light and fluffy. Beat in eggs, one at a time, beating well after each egg. Stir in vanilla, zucchini, raisins with liquid and orange rind. Sift dry ingredients; add to zucchini mixture. stirring until well blended. Fold in nuts. Bake in a 9X13 pan 350 for 1 hr. Dust with powdered sugar.

Mexican Milk Cake

This recipe comes from Mexico but other countries make cakes like this, too. Why is it different? It's just a butter cake. What makes it unusual is that after it is baked, the cake is soaked with a mixture of three different milk products. Then it's refrigerated. When it's served, it is usually topped with frosting, whipped cream, fruit or nuts. But not all of them.

1 1/2 cups flour	Preheat oven to 350.
1 tsp. baking powder	Grease and flour a 9 X 13 inch baking pan.
1/2 cup unsalted butter	
1 cup white sugar	Sift flour and baking powder together and set aside.
5 eggs	
1/2 tsp. vanilla	Cream butter and cup of sugar together until fluffy.
1 cup milk	Add eggs and vanilla. Beat well. Add the flour mixture several tablespoons at a time, mixing well until blended. Pour batter into prepared pan. Bake 30 minutes. Cool cake.
1/2 of a 14-ounce can Sweetened Condensed milk	
1/2 of a 12-ounce can Evaporated milk	

Pierce cooled cake 8 to 10 times with a fork and let it cool a little more. Combine the milks and pour over top

My Secret Mashed Potatoes

If you live in the country, weather is important. The two Canadian radio stations in Trail, BC. nail it more often than the Internet. Global warming is real. When the first cookbook was written in the early 1990's, we had two weeks in the summer that were over ninety degrees. The last few years, temperatures have been in the '90's, often over 100, starting in July and going into September. Months of such heat mean drought conditions: more evergreens will die from bark beatles, fire conditions will be elevated, limits to logging in the forests will be set and there is absolutely no burning. In this season, the major weather risk in mountains is fire. This must compensate for the fact that there are few, if any, snakes, earthquakes or tornadoes here.

10 large Russet potatoes	In saucepan over high heat, bring potatoes to boil in
Water	salted water.
1 tsp. salt	Reduce to medium and simmer 15 minutes or until
1 Tbsp. baking soda	fork easily goes through.
1/2 cup hot milk	Drain. Add baking soda, butter and sour cream.
4 Tbsp. sour cream	
4 Tbsp. butter	Beat with enough hot milk to a fluffy consistency.

Party Crunch

Laura Rinard, my California niece shows her Collies in dog shows and recently fulfilled another dream when she bought an Arabian horse. She has a refreshingly, wicked sense of humor and so do her friends. Laura invited me to one of their monthly Bunko games and we laughed the night away. And, pigged out on this Crunch. It arrived in a huge bowl and although there was a lot of other food, too, it had all been eaten by twelve women when the evening was over.

1/2 box Chex cereal	Toast almonds and set aside.
1/2 box Wheat Chex cereal	Toast coconut and set that aside, too.
1/2 box Golden Grahams	Pour cereals into large bowl. Add almonds and coconut.
1/2 bag shredded coconut	
1/2 bag almonds (sliced, slivered or whole)	In saucepan, boil sugar, butter and Karo for 5 minutes. Remove from heat and pour over mix.
1 cup light Karo syrup	
1 cup sugar	Stir with wooden spoon to get thoroughly mixed. Let sit for five minutes to harden.
1 stick butter	

Pastry

There's a subtle difference in the texture and patina of a pastry made from scratch in the home kitchen. The color appears sweeter, more delicate, the crust, lighter, more tender and flaky. There aren't many ingredients in pastry: flour, oil and water, but each has many options. Shall it be wheat or white flour, butter, lard or Crisco? Lard makes a tender crust, butter a more crisp, brown crust. Lightness of the pasty depends upon the amount of air enclosed, and the expansion of that air in baking. Flakiness depends upon the number of layers of shortening and flour formed by folding and rolling. Handle pastry as little as possible.

2 1/2 cups white flour

1/4 cup butter

1/4 cup lard

1 tsp. sugar

1 tsp. salt

5 Tbsp. (about) ice water

Sift together the salt, sugar & flour. Cut in the butter & lard with knife or by hand until the size of peas.

Add ice water gradually, until all is moistened. Sprinkle flour onto board. Flour the rolling Take a handful of pastry and roll from center out. Note:Brush uncrust with water around edges to prevent shrinkage.

Peanut Butter Fingers

In early December, Elva Willingham and her husband, Don, were to visit the Lazy Bee. Martha and Alice, our neighbors, were hosting a cookie exchange at that time and they invited Elva, too. As she was making cookies in Spokane, Don asked "How many?"so many times until she finally understood what he was saying. She'd answer, "Nine," but then he'd repeat the question. Finally, she got it. "It's only for women, Don. You're not invited." We made four cookies each for the nine persons attending Happily, Don got to sample all of the yummy cookies after the exchange. Was this cookie made by Kathleen, Merrilyn, Leesa, Judy, Deena, Alice, Lenore, Martha or Elva? It wasn't mine.

1 cup sugar	Prehat oven to 350 degrees.
1 cup butter	
1 cup brown sugar	Cream peanut butter and sugars.
2 eggs	
2/3 cup peanut butter	Add eggs and peanut butter. Stir
1 tsp. baking soda	until smooth. Add remaining
1/2 tsp. salt	ingredients except topping. Mix
1 tsp. vanilla	well. Put in a greased 9 X 13 pan.
2 cups flour	Press mixture down evenly.
2 cups oatmeal	Bake 20 minute & remove from oven.
TOPPING:	Cover immediately with choc. chips.
12 oz chocolate chips	Let them melt, then spread evenly.
1/2 cup powdered sugar	Blend rest of topping together. Spread
1/4 cup peanut butter	evenly over melted chips, making
2-4 Tbsp. milk	swiwling pattern. Cool.

57

Pear Crumble Pie

Nancy Folkestad received this recipe from Gail Jones years ago when they both worked in the same dental office. "We keep in touch even though the years and moves have separated us. We recently got together in Chewelah." Nancy uses fresh pears, various kinds she gets at Sherman Orchards. She especially likes Bartletts. "I tell the doneness by how the juice looks, how brown the topping is and the feel of the pears to a paring knife." This pie is so unique and appealing that when I arrived late to a meeting, three people whispered to me that I should get some of her pear pie. Nancy says the recipe won't work if you use canned.

Unbaked pie crust
6 to 7 medium fresh pears
2 to 3 Tbsp. lemon juice
1/2 cup sugar
2 Tbsp. flour
1 tsp. lemon zest

Crumble Topping
1/2 cup flour
1/2 cup sugar
1/2 tsp. ginger
1/2 tsp. cinnamon
1/4 tsp. mace
1/4 cup butter
For topping, cut in butter
to all ingredients till crumbly.

Sprinkle pears with lemon juice.

Mix sugar, flour, lemon zest, then mix in the pears and spoon into an unbaked pie crust. Sprinkle with topping. Preheat oven to 400. Turn down to 325 and bake about one hour, testing for doneness.

Pigs in Blankets

A few years ago, there was a rash of cougar attacks on people. A two-day seminar about cougars, or mountain lions as they're often known, was held near Colville. It was presented by the Mountain Lion Society headquartered in California. There we learned, by a show of hands, that the majority of people who have actually seen these illusive critters live in the Northport area or by us near the Canadian border. That's because these powerful animals have trails between the U.S. and Canada for cross breeding. Some years they roam here and then disappear, perhaps like this very old hor d'hourves recipe.

2 eight ounce cans quick cresent dinner rolls

2 Tbsp. Dijon or honey mustard

1 sixteen-ounce jar cocktail franks or cut-to-fit hotdogs

(These can be made ahead and frozen until needed. To reheat, thaw on cookie sheets covered with foil, baked 350 about 10 min.)

Preheat oven to 375.

Separate dough into 8 triangles. Cut each triangle into thirds lengthwise and spread with mustard, then place the hotdogs on the wide end and roll up tightly.

Place on ungreased cookie sheets, point down. Bake 12-15 min. until golden brown.

Raspberry Cream Pie

A rugged outdoorsman can be as romantic as any female. Several men have told us they'd like to be married at the Lazy Bee. One rainy June day, we found a note from one of the fellows on the Silvertip Forestry crew. It said, "We want to be married here June 24th". The bridal party soon returned. The bride decided that the bridal procession would walk between the two raised flower beds and go across the lawn between the seated guests to meet the pastor, groom and attendants where trees form a canopy overhead. Shenna Rose and Richard Lembcke's dream came true at 6 p.m. just as the sun was setting. This is the sort of pie that may have been at their wedding buffet at Colville Eagles Lodge.

Graham cracker crust

1 1/3 cup sugar

6 Tbsp. cornstarch

1 1/8 tsp. salt

1 1/2 cup water (two if using fresh berries

4 Tbsp corn syrup

12 oz. frozen raspberries or 1 pint fresh

Mix sugar, cornstarch, salt. Add 1/2 cup water and berries. Cook over medium heat until thick, stirring constantly. Set aside to cool. While cooking make cream filling:

4 ounce soft cream cheese
1/2 cup sugar
5 ounce whipped topping

Fold cream cheese, sugar & topping together. Spoon over crust. Spoon cooled berry filling over cream mix and chill for 2 hrs.

Really Yummy Baked Beans

Judy and Ted Martin were having a potluck. "I'm letting everyone tell me what they want to bring," she said. "But I'm hoping you'll make baked beans. It's an old-fashioned dish and I know you'll have a good recipe." Indeed, I did. This is the best I've found. It's not as great as the one that a guest brought to the Broughton's potluck. Selma, a friend from Montana, came with us to that one. Apparently, she liked those baked beans. She went back several times and filled her plate with them, until finally she brought the serving pot back to the table and set it right in front of her. Now that's a tacky but supreme compliment!

1 large onion, chopped

1 large green pepper, chopped

1/2 tsp. ketchup

2 Tbsp. honey

2 Tbsp. brown sugar

1/4 tsp. Worchestershire Sauce

Chopped, crisp bacon

1 can prepared pork & beans

Saute onion and green pepper in ketchup.

Blend in honey, brown sugar, Worchestershire sauce and chopped bacon.

Add pork and beans.

Cook on low heat, stirring occasionally, until liquid is absorbed.

Double ingredients if more beans are desired.

Remarkable Scones

One spring not too long ago, Alice Hauflin and I decided to have a series of High Teas during the summer. Our husbands thought we were crazy. One of them said, "Who's going to drive all the way up here and pay almost twenty dollars for tea and crumpets?" Each tea was a sell-out. Bud wore his black tie jacket, a top hat and jeans. With a rifle slung over the handlebars of his Honda motrocycle, he parked guest cars out-of-sight. The teas went on for three hours, classical music playing in the background. Lenore Whyte and Alice waitressed the tables in long, black skirts and starched white blouses. I kept busy making two kinds of tea for the huge antique cups, everyone drinking at least seven cups, and making sure these scones came out of the oven on time.

1 1/2 cups white flour

4 tsp. baking powder

5 Tbsp. butter

5 Tbsp. sugar

2/3 cup milk

1 egg yolk, lightly beaten

Flavor with apple bits, cherries, and/or pecans.

Sift flour & baking powder. Rub butter and sugar into flour to form fine crumbles. Make well in center. Add milk & optional flavorings. Knead gently together but don't over mix. Roll out on floured surface to 3/8 inch and cut out scones with cookie cutter. Place on greased baking sheet and brush tops with egg yok. Bake 12-15 minutes until lightly golden. Serve with Lemon Curd, page 51.

Rhubarb-Apple Deep Dish Pie

Country food is daily fare. It's all about real food rather than out-of-season rarities. Prized is freshly-gathered vegetables, fruits and newly-baked breads or casseroles. Nothing better than rhubarb pie, unless it's apple pie. Combine the two for this bottom-crusted version.

2 lbs. rhubarb (8 cups)	**Set oven to 400. Prepare pastry.**
4 large Granny Smith apples	**Trim and cut rhubarb into 1-inch pieces. Peel core and cut each apple into 12 wedges**
1 1/2 cups sugar	
14 cup cornstarch	**In large saucepan, put sugar, cornstarch and**
1 tsp. cinnamon	**cinnamon until well mixed. Stir in apples,**
2 Tlbs. butter	**butter and lemen juice. Let stand 5 min., then**
1 Tbsp. lemon juice	**cover & cook over med low heat until apples**
Pastry (see recipe else-in this cookbook)	**soften. Remove from heat. Stir in rhubarb. Cool. Fill deep dish with pastry, then filling. Brush pastry top with milk. Bake 55 min.**

Rhubarb-Cranberry Cobbler

So few seem to enjoy ironing. This repetitive task can be so soothing. It's easy once you get in the mood and set up the ironing board, or a towel on a tabletop if you don't have a board. **Here's how to iron a shirt in two minutes:** Lay out shirt over board. Iron collar. Lift shirt and iron each sleeve in turn. Then place the back of the garment on the board. Iron the inside of the back. Place each half of the shirt front over the back and iron. Do the other half.. You're done. Now, you've got time to make this dish.

2 cups sugar	**Set oven to 350. Butter 13 X 9 X 2 baking dish.**
3 1/2 Tbsp. cornstarch	
1/4 teaspoon cinnamon	
1/4 teaspoon ground ginger	**Whisk 1 cup sugar, cinnamon, corn starch & ginger in large bowl. Mix in rhubarb, cranberries and juice. Put in dish and bake for about 30 min. 'till bubbly. Beat butter & sugar in bowl 'till blended. Beat in egg, then vanilla & milk. Sift the flour, salt & baking powder. Add and blend. Drop by Tbsps. on hot fruit & bake 45 min.**
8 cups frozen rhubarb or 2 lbs. unthawed	
1 cup fresh or frozen cranberries	
1/4 cup cranberry juice	
1/2 cup butter, room temp.	
1 large egg	
1 tsp. vanilla	
1/2 cup milk	
1 cup flour	
1 teaspoon baking powder	
1/4 teaspoon salt	
Vanilla ice cream	

Rhubarb-Strawberry Cobbler

Spring is just around the corner. Neighbors have sighted robins. But, it just keeps snowing. The sky shows no sign that the white stuff will ever stop coming down. Last Sunday, to relieve everyone's anxiety about the condition of the highway, we decided to re-schedule an event. I used to feel disappointment when something like that happened. Now I feel it just made way for something even better. So, why not think about things to do with rhubarb this spring!

3 cups rhubarb, cut in 1/2 inch
    pieces
2/3 cup sugar
1 Tbsp. orange peel
1 Tbsp. butter
1 Tbsp. flour
3 cups sliced strawberries

For batter:
1 3/4 cup flour
1 Tbsp. baking powder
1/2 tsp. salt
6 Tbsp. butter, chilled
1/2 cup, plus 2 Tbsp. sugar
3/4 cup half and half
2 Tbsp. orange zest

Set oven to 425. Put sugar, rhubarb and orange peel in a saucepan. Heat over medium heat until rhubarb begins to render its juices, about 2 min. Add butter & flour & bring to boil and stir constantly for 1 min. Remove from heat. Add the strawberries & pour into 10-inch oven-proof pie dish. Sift flour, baking powder & salt together. Cut butter in & make coarse crumbs. Blend in 1/2 cup sugar. Blend in 1/2 and 1/2 with a fork. Spoon dough over fruit in dish. Combine 2 Tbsp. sugar & zest & put on top. Bake 25-30 min.

65

Ritz Cracker Dessert

Tricia Woods was a professional volunteer when she first arrived in Colville. Now she uses her vast supply of energy to promoting Colville as its Office Manager. As a member, the Lazy Bee receives weekly reports from the Chamber president of the varied activities taking place in the Colville Valley. The Chamber office is located behind the gorgeous clock statue on Main Street. If you need to know who's who, or who's got what, Tricia can rattle off phone numbers for businesses or individuals without looking them up. She even gives local weather reports to pilots. When Bud was returning from Yakima and needed to know what the ceiling was like over Mingo Mountain, Tricia went outside and told him.

30 Ritz crackers, rolled fine
1/4 cup butter

Melt butter & mix with finely-rolled Ritz crackers. Pat in a 9 X 9 inch pan.

Filling:
4 egg whites, beaten
4 egg yolks, beaten
1/2 cup sugar
1 small can crushed
 pineapple and its juices
1/2 package lemon jello,
 made with 1 cup hot
 water

For filling add 1/4 cup sugar to 4 beaten egg yolks, can pineapple & juices. Then add egg whites beaten with 1/4 cup sugar. Add the hot jello. Pour over crust. Refrigerate. Serve with whipped creeam.

Scotch Broth Soup

When you open your doors to bed and breakfast guests, you often make lifelong friends. Minnesota Jo Ann Groth and her husband Jim, now residents of Colville, became two of ours. Jo Ann introduced me to the premier farmgirl, Maryjane Butters of Moscow, ID. A rural Martha Stewart, MJ gives women worldwide ideas for home, garden and decorating. When we were guests of the Groths, we brought them a quart of this hearty soup. Jim liked it so much, Jo Ann asked for the recipe and soon had a pot of it brewing for two days on top of the wood stove in their livingroom.

2 pounds meaty beef bones	**In a large kettle combine bones & water. Simmer**
6 quarts water	**1 1/2 hours or until meat falls off bones.**
2 cups chopped carrots	
2 cups chopped turnips	**Remove bones, chill and strain. Skim off fat.**
2 cups chopped celery	**Remove meat from bones. Dice meat. Add**
1 cup chopped onion	**to broth along with vegetables and barley.**
8 ounces peral barley	**Bring to boil, then simmer l hr. or more till ingredients are tender.**

67

Simple Walnut Bread

Julie Jordon taught us how to die with humor, grace and dignity. During one of the last weeks of her short life, we drove over to have lunch with her and her daughter in a cabin that perched on the side of a mountain above the Gifford Ferry. She had a queen's view of the valley and river below. In her tiny kitchen that had open shelving holding glass jars, she pranced about making this simple walnut bread as if she had no serious concerns. Her recipe makes one loaf pan of delicious bread. It toasts to a golden hue and has the lingering taste of walnuts.

2 Tbsp. honey

1 Tbsp. molasses

1 cup warm water

1 packet yeast

2 1/2 cup flour

1 cup whole walnuts

1/2 cup sesame seeds

Fill a bowl with 1 cup warm water. Add yeast, honey and molasses. Let sit a few minutes and then add flour and beat with vigor until dough is well blended.

Unearth onto floured board and knead until dough is elastic and no additional flour can be added. Cover with damp cloth and let stand until twice the size. Place in greased pan. Cover again and let stand 1 hr. before baking in 400 oven 30 min. or until toothpick comes out clean.

Slow-Cooker Beef Stew

What recipe is calling you? Cooking can be an inner journey and soulful advernutre. Why not venture into the unknown with the knowledge that you are giving meaning to the creation your hands are making? You are preparing a dish that shows your love for those for whom you cook. A good cook is not intent upon arriving, just experiencing the moment. The joy of creating awaits. Does this dish appeal to you?

1 3 lb. chuck roast	Rub meat with salt and pepper. Heat a heavy skillet over medium heat. Coat pan with spray. Cook roast in pan 10 minutes, browning on both sides.
1 tsp. salt	
Cooking spray	
1/4 cup water	Remove from pan. Add 1/4 cup water to pan and stir to loosen browned bits. Add onion and parsnips. Saute 5 min. or until veggies are tender.
2 cups onions, sliced vertically (1 large)	
1 1/2 cups chopped parsnips (about 2)	Place onion mixture, vinegar, bay leaf and beer in large slow cooker. Cover & cook on LOW for 8 hours. Discard bay leaf. Cut up meat. Serve with sauce.
1 Tbsp. balsamic vinegar	
1 bay leaf	
1 bottle beer	

Slow-Roasted 5- Star Pork

Here's how a six- to seven-pound port butt roast (shoulder roast) can become fragrant and fork-tender in 8 1/2 to 10 1/2 hours. First, it's seared and rubbed with herbs. While it is baking, the aromas throughout the cooking day are heavenly. In Italy, it's known as Porchetta. The meat seems to melt as the juices drips off. Directions continue on the next page.

10 cloves garlic, peeled

1/2 cup fennel seeds

2 Tbsp. coarse sea salt

1/2 tsp. black pepper

5 to 6 small dried red chiles, crumbled, with the seeds

1 boneless pork shoulder butt (about 6-7 lb.)

1/2 cup hot water

Juice of 1 lemon

1/2 cup chicken broth

Heat to 450 degrees.

Crush garlic & fennel seeds. Mix them with salt, pepper & chilies.

Cut 1-inch slits all over roast, including the bottom. Rub garlic-seed mixture into slits.

Heat 2 Tbsp. olive oil in heavy roast pan. Sear meat on all sides 10-12 minutes but don't let garlic burn.

Remove roast from pan (Pleasecontinue on the opposite page.)

Continued Directions 5-Star Pork

This appears more complex than it is. Just assemble the ingredients and follow the directions on both pages to achieve a masterful meat. If you try to get by with a smaller pork butt than 6-7 pounds, it won't turn out the same. It has to be big to get the distinct smells and flavors by the slow roast process. I know, I tried this method with a smaller roast and was sadly disappointed. Both bone in and bone-out are equally good, but bone-out is easier to find. If you use bone-in, bake for another hour.

After roast has been removed, add the hot water and stir and deglaze (means to scrape up all the meat bits).

Add a rack, if you have one, in bottom of the pan. I wrap a trivet with foil and place the roast on it. Put meat in fatty side up and put in oven UNCOVERED 30 minutes.

Pour lemon juice and chicken broth over meat. Brush 2 Tbsp. olive oil over roast.

Reduce heat to 250 degrees.

Cover pan and baste occasionally with pan juice during the 8 to 10 hours it slowly bakes.

The roast is done when the meat falls apart when touched with a fork. The exquisite pan juices become the gravy.
71

Snazzy Cranberries

A Rocking Chair Chat was put on by the Keller Museum
Several old-time residents sat in rocking chairs and told
how life used to be in this area. Travel to Colville from the
Deep Lake area in the 1920's and 30's, they said, took two
days and folks stayed at a half-way house. Too much time
had gone by so no one could recall the details of how that
was done. After WWII, many families pulled up stakes
and left the area, encouraged by easier transportation and
the money to be made in big cities. Now that land prices
are no longer cheap in Montana or Idaho, rural land in
Washington, especially in Stevens County, is being re-dis
covered. These stories hopefully will bring a taste of the
life they seek. Here's my new version for cranberries.

Package of cranberries	**Prepare cranberries according to directions on the package.**
2 cups water	**Remove from stove to cool.**
1 cup sugar	
1 small apple, in chunks	**Put apple chunks and raisins in cranberry juice and heat 'till apples are soft.**
1/2 cup juice from bottled cranberry juice	**Add the walnuts.**
1/2 cup raisins	**Add to the cool cranberries.**
1/2 cup whole walnuts	**You can also add orange bits, tiny marshmallows, olives.**

Chicken So Good I Stole The Recipe

My recipes come from friends, newspapers, Internet, restaurants and Mother's red recipe box. But this one was stolen. It happened at a barber shop in Canada. Bud was having his hair cut by a frail woman barber. He was the sole customer. Piles of outdated magazines were stacked in three rows in front of the big windows. I found this recipe in one of the magazines. They were deep in conversation. I didn't have pen or paper. Surely she won't miss this page. So I ripped. The sound echoed through the tiny space. "What are you doing?" she yelled. I looked at her and pled, "Just a little recipe," and then got up to show her the page in the magazine. "Looks good," she agreed. So six to eight persons will love chicken made this way. It gets five stars and you tell me if it was worth the risk.

Set oven to 425 degrees

1/4 cup chopped fresh
    oregano or cilantro

4 cloves garlic, chopped

2 Tbsp. fresh lemon zest

1/4 cup extra virgin
    olive oil

1 roaster chicken, about
    six pounds

Blend oregano, garlic, and
    zest with oilve oil

Season bird inside and
    with salt and pepper

Rub 1/2 oil mixture inside
    and outside of bird

Roast 15 minutes and then
    reduce to 325 for
    1 hr and 15 minutes

Let chicken rest 15 min.
    before carving

Spaghetti Sauce

Martha Johnson, our exercise cheerleader, lives up the road from the Lazy Bee. That's not her only talent. She's an exceptional mechanic who helps her husband, Larry, rebuild Stearman biplanes. Martha organizes daily walking groups, cross-country ski forays and summer kayak treks. She's the kind of gal who can love every windy minute sitting in an open cockpit plane for 18 hours flying from the Midwest across the mountains to their landing strip in the Forgotten Corner. A gracious hostess and a good cook, she shares her recipe for Italian spaghetti sauce.

1 lb. pork sausage, ground
2 lb. ground round
4 large onions, chopped
4-6 garlic cloves, minced
1 cup parsley, chopped
3/4 lbs. fresh mushrooms
3 cans (15 oz.) tomato sauce
4/5 quart dry red wine
2 tsp. salt
1 tsp. sage
1 tsp. rosemary
1/2 tsp marjoram
1/2 tsp. thyme
1/2 tsp. pepper

In large kettle or dutch oven, slowly brown the sausage and ground round.
Remove meat to dish. To kettle add onions and saute until limp. Add garlic, parsley and mushrooms and stir to coat meat drippings. Stir in remaining ingredients.

Put meat back into pot. Cover loosely and simmer for three hours. Stir occasionally. Skim off fat.

(Makes 3 quarts)

74

Spinach with Sesame Seeds

If we haven't been to a home before, or if he's forgotten, Bud asks, "Do I take my shoes off, or can I leave them on?" He'll wear slip-ons if shoes are requested to come off before entering. If not, he wears hiking or cowboy boots. Creative house guests come with slippers. Ones that look made like bunny rabbits, frogs, cows or Disney characters are especially welcome. Carry in this dish and the hostess won't care what shoes you're wearing. (Maybe)

1 lb. washed spinach, roots and stem bottoms removed

2 1/2 Tbsp. toasted sesame seeds that are chopped

1 1/2 tsp. sugar

1 12/ tsp. soy sauce

Pinch of salt

Toast sesame seeds in a pan over low heat. then chop.

Blanch spinach in boiling water for 30 seconds. Drain. Refresh under cold water.

Gently squeeze to release excess water.

Combine sesame seeds, sugar and soy sauce in small bowl. Cut spinach in one-inch pieces and squeeze out any excess water and place in bowl. Pour over sesame mixture and toss well.

Sticky Rolls

This makes twenty HUGE rolls. Wait for a warm day to make a yeast product if you live in the mountains. (Please see following page for the remainder of directions. It's not all that complicated but takes a lot of explaining.)

1/2 cup warm water	In a small bowl combine water, yeast and sugar.
2 packages dry yeast	Stir until dissolved. Set aside.
2 Tbsp. sugar	
3 1/2 ounce package vanilla pudding	In a large bowl, make pudding according to package directions. Add margarine, eggs & salt and mix well. Then add yeast mixture.
1/2 cup margarine, melted	
2 eggs	
1 tsp. salt	Gradually add flour. Knead until smooth.
6 cups flour	Place in greased bowl. Cover with damp cloth and let rise until double
1 cup soft butter	
2 cups brown sugar	Punch down and let rise again. (See further directions next page).
4 tsp. cinnamon	

More About Making Sticky Rolls

To let a yeast product rise, place in a warm spot in a room with no drafts. Or, you can place these covered rolls to rise in a pre-heated warm oven that has a pan of hot water placed on the shelf beneath it. (This page continues directions to make sticky rolls.)

Roll out dough onto a floured board. Take 1 cup of the softened butter and spread over the surface.

In a small bowl, mix two cups brown sugar and the four teaspoons of cinnamon. Sprinkle this mixture over the rolled-out dough.

Tightly roll up dough. With a knife, notch and cut dough into two inch pieces.

Place on lightly-greased cookie sheets two inches apart.

Press down each roll with your hand. Cover again with a damp cloth and let rise.

Bake in a 350 degree oven for 15 to 20 minutes. Don't overbake. Remove when they turn a light golden brown.

Stir Fry Sauce

When I'm slicing fresh gingerroot for this recipe, I recall the free-lance article I wrote for an Iowa newspaper about a ginseng collector entitled, "Secrets of a Ginseng Hunter." Ginseng roots resemble fresh gingerroot, or vise versa. It was a very exciting interview. I was pledged to secrecy about how he sold the roots in China and where he was finding the wild plants in Iowa A slice of gingerroot in a pitcher of water, incidentally, might relieve gas pains.

6 Tbsp. cornstarch

2 1/2 Tbsp. beef bouillon

3/4 tsp. onion powder

6 Tbsp. wine vinegar

2 Tbsp. grated fresh
     gingerroot

1 Tbsp. garlic, finely minced

2 2/3 cup vinegar

3/4 cup dark corn syrup

In small bowl, combine bouillon & onion powder with the wine vinegar.

Then add the freshly grated gingerroot, garlic, corn syrup and other type of vinegar.

(Try this and see if you like it as well or better than the store bought.)

Strawberry Nut Bread

We know spring is here because Bud's pressure-washing the decks. As we put furniture back in place, we run across the mosquito-repellant candles. Mosquitos, bees or wasps are annoying and some people are allergic to their sting. The good news, however, is that comfrey plants are growing by the house. If bitten, you can break off a bit of a wide leaf, chew it to get it moistened, and then place it on the spot. The buzz goes away. If another jolt is needed to relieve the unpleasant feeling, a bit of Tea Tree oil can do the trick, or a piece of the aloe vera houseplant, or taking time to eat some of this delicious bread just out the oven.

1 package (16 ounces) unsweetened whole strawberries, thawed & drained
1 3/4 cups sugar
1 1/4 cups vegetable oil
4 eggs
3 cups flour
2 tsp. cinnamon
1 tsp. baking soda
1 tsp. salt
1 cup chopped walnuts

Heat oven to 350. Grease bottoms of 2 loaf pans. Slightly mash berries in in large bowl with fork. Stir in sugar, oil & eggs until well blended. Stir in other ingredients except walnuts until moistened. Stir in walnuts. Pour into pans.

Bake 50 to 55 minutes or until toothpick in center comes out clean. Cool 5 minutes before removing from pans.

Stuffed Pumpkin or Squash

What ingiues us to try the new and leave the familiar behind? On a cook's journey through life, the first time a dish is made, each success or failure leads to new discoveries. So, if you go with an impulse to create a new dish like this, it might bring about new wonders. Helen Keller said, "Life is either a daring adventure or nothing." Why not have an pumpkin adventure?

1 pumpkin or squash
1 Tbsp. brown sugar
1/2 stick butter
1 Tbsp. oil
2 onions, finely
   chopped
1 clove garlic, crushed
1 cup ground beef
2 cup pine nuts
1/2 cup slivered
   almonds
1/3 cup dried or fresh
   dates, chopped
1 tsp. cinnamon
1 cup cooked rice
Salt & pepper

Cut stlk end off pumpkin or squash to use as its lid.

Scoop out seeds and fiber. Spread brown sugar inside the pumpkin with a wood spoon.

Melt butter in large fry pan & brown onions. Add the garlic and ground meat & brown. In a sauce pan, toast pine nuts & almonds. Use NO oil. Just move pan to prevent them from scorching. Add nuts, dates, cinnamon and rice to meat.

(Fill pumpkin with meat mixture and fit top back on. Put on a cookie sheet and bake at 375 for at least 1 hour or 'till pumpkin is soft.)

Tuna Casserole

Simple blessings. Count them one by one. I'm singing the old gospel hymn as I'm plucking up forest debris and tossing it into a wheelbarrow, chanting, "Phone call from one of the ten children." Then, singing out names of the grandchildren, I pause to appreciate the beauty of the forest around me and add, "Fragrance of fresh lavender. . .Spirited game of tennis or cribbage. . .Hairy, the ancient cat following me. . .Early light of dawn. . . .The first snow. . . Reading a thrilling adventure novel." Heading back now to dump these branches and make this casual casserole for a hearty lunch.

3 1/2 ounces chow mein noodles	**Set oven to 350.**
1/2 cup water	**In a big bowl, combine all the ingredients.**
2 cans of tuna, well drained	**Bake uncovered in a greased casserole dish**
1 cup cashew nuts	**for one hour.**
1 cup celery, chopped	
1/4 cup onion, minced	
Dash pepper	

Yogurt Mint Cooler

(These comments are not about food but rather the spirit of a place.) Teenagers were overheard at Colville McDonald's. "McDonald's is a cool place." I wanted to jump into their conversation to say, "I've known that for years. It's a place where I've been able to jumpstart my creative juices many times. There's something subtle about the ambience. Perhaps, it's the bright lighting or the fact that it attracts all ages, from senior men enjoying a coffee klatch in a corner booth, to two people conducting business, to several who are reading the free newspapers, or Moms bringing in kids. To me, it offers freedom. You can stop by just to use their restrooms, or to leisurely sit in a booth and have no one looking over your shoulder. In fact, I wrote this little essay there the other night on a napkin before a bridge game while sipping a cup of coffee.

1 cup plain yogurt

2 cups cold milk

6 springs fresh spearmint or peppermint, chopped & crushed

2 Tbsp. honey

Stir together or mix in a blender.

(The protein in the yogurt makes this almost a meal in a glass.)

Zucchini Quiche

At the Waneta Border Crossing into Canada, there's a store with heart. Richard and Betty, the owners, not only supply gas and propane, UPS and mail boxes, hot and tasty hotdogs, Lottery tickets and groceries but they're an important communications link for the community. Need to sell something, put it on the bulletin board and tell Richard. He'll know someone who's looking. Trying to find a neighbor who should be home but isn't, ask Betty. She might know where they've gone. Need a book to read. The Rural Library has a small on-your-honor paperback collection to which store customers have supplemented with so many books that Richard has had to build more shelving. I miss the cribbage games that used to go on there just as much I miss having enough zucchini to make this casserole. Squirrels carry mine away.

3 cups zucchini, shredded
4 eggs, lightly beaten
1 cup packaged biscuit mix
1/2 cup grated Parmesan cheese
2 ounces Gruyere or Swiss
     cheese, shredded
1/4 cup cooking oil
1 onion, chopped
2 Tbsp. cilantro, chopped

Preheat oven to 350.

In a large bowl, combine all the ingredients.

Pour into a greased 9-inch quiche dish or large pie tin.

Bake uncovered for 40-45 minutes until knife inserted near the center comes out clean.

83

Too Good
To Be Forgotten
Recipes

**Featuring Americana Basics
from the
Northwest Mountains**

*Please enjoy these recipes from
Out - of print first edition.*

Menu Ideas from the First Edition

Breakfast
Brunch Eggs
Ham on top Stove
Rhubarb Muffins

Lunch
Flavorful Onion Soup
French Bread
Orange Salad
Lazy Bee Sugar Cookies

Dinner
Baked Chicken Casserole
Honey-glazed Carrots
Waldorf Salad
French Bread
Sour Cream Apple Pie

Apple Dumplings

I tuck this recipe in my suitcase when I visit my children and their families. They like apple dumplings almost as much as rhubarb crisp. Little children like to help fold the apples into their blankets of dough and pour the syrup over them.

2 cups water

1 *1/2* cups sugar

1/2 tsp. cinnamon

1/2 tsp. nutmeg

1/4 cup butter

2 *1/4* cups flour

2 tsp. baking powder

2/3 cup shortening

1/2 cup milk

6 small apples, peeled
  and cored
1/3 cup sugar

COMBINE 1 *1/2* cups sugar, *1/4* teaspoon of the cinnamon, *1/4* teaspoon of the nutmeg, and two cups water in a saucepan and bring to boil. Reduce heat and cook five minutes. Remove from heat and stir in butter. Set aside.

COMBINE flour, baking powder and *1/2* teaspoon salt. Cut in shortening until mixture is course crumbs. Add milk all at once. Stir just until all is moistened. Roll into a ball.

ON a floured surface, roll out into an 18x12-inch rectangle. Cut into six squares of about six inches.

PLACE a pealed and cored apple in the center of each square. Sprinkle apples with mixture of *1/3* cups sugar and remaining *1/4* teaspoon each of cinnamon and nutmeg. Dot with additional butter.

MOISTEN edges of dough; fold corners to center atop apple. Pinch edges together. Place in a large baking dish. Pour syrup over dumplings.

BAKE in a 375 degree oven for 45 minutes or until apples are tender

Apple or Rhubarb Crisp

Keep an ear peeled for neighbors who have rhubarb to give away. Freshly picked rhubarb makes a better crisp. Cut the rhubarb or apples into chunks about one inch, and put into greased baking dish. I like to freeze several and bake one for eating. Don't bake if freezing. Label the container: Thaw. Bake. 350 degrees for I hour. If baking without thawing, then it may take longer than a hour.

5 cups diced fruit

GREASE a 9 X 13 pan.

1 cup white sugar

Place diced fruit in bottom of pan. Make mixture of sugar, flour and cinnamon and sprinkle on top.

1 Tbsp. flour

1 tsp. cinnamon

TOP:

MIX up topping and sprinkle over fruit.

3/4 cup oatmeal

BAKE in 350 degree oven until brown, about 35 minutes.

3/4 cup flour

3/4 cup brown sugar

1/3 cup melted butter

1/4 tsp. soda

1/4 tsp. baking powder

Baked Chicken Casserole

It's hard to believe, but the longer the chicken in this recipe bakes, the better it will be. After baking this dish tbe required time, it can keep another hour with the oven turned off. Cook it one or two hours in a 325 degree oven. This is a good dish to have in the oven if you're not sure how long you'll have to hold the dinner meal. This is another recipe from the South.

Frying chicken

4 Tbsp. butter

1 Tbsp. flour

1/2 pint whip cream, unwhipped

Can sliced mushrooms

Salt/pepper

Cup white, dry wine

CUT up chicken. Melt four tablespoons butter in large baking pan or casserole dish. Add cut-up chicken.

SPRINKLE flour over chicken pieces. Mix cream, unwhipped, with mushrooms, salt and pepper to taste, and a cup of white, dry wine and pour over chicken.

BAKE in 325 degree oven for one to two hours.

Baked Summer Squash

I didn't know a summer squash from a spring squash, nor did I care until I tasted this famous dish at Aunt Fanny's Restaurant in Atlanta, GA. Then, I returned to Spokane to find summer squash to make the dish, and learned that summer squash is long and yellow, with a little crook neck .This is hauntingly sweet and goes well with corn bread and fried chicken. In a phone conversation with Gratna Poole, manager of Aunt Fanny's who gave permission to reprint the recipe, she said millions had enjoyed the casserole during the years the restaurant has been open and many more had loved it before that when Aunt Fanny originated and cooked the casserole on a Georgia plantation.

3 Lbs. yellow summer squash

1/2 cup chopped onions

1/2 cup cracker meal or bread crumbs

1 tsp. salt

1/2 tsp. black pepper (increase salt and pepper to suit your taste)

2 eggs

1 Tbsp. sugar

1 stick butter, melted

WASH and cut up unpeeled squash. Boil until tender, draining thoroughly, then mash with fork.

ADD all ingredients except 1/2 of the butter to the squash.

POUR squash mixture into a greased baking dish. Spread the remaining melted butter on the top and sprinkle with cracker meal or bread crumbs.

BAKE in 375 degree oven for about one hour or until brown on top.

89

Barbecue Sauce Marinade

When it's summer, it's time to barbecue. Place cut-up meat in a 9x 13-inch pan, covering with marinade which will then be used to baste the meat on the grill. Refrigerate over night so marinade soaks into meat. Brush marinade over meat with each turn on the grill. For the final coating, use a heavy, commercial barbecue sauce. This makes finger-licking good barbecue.

3 cloves garlic. crushed

COMBINE ingredients and simmer for 15 minutes.

1/3 cup vegetable oil

USE as marinade and then brush marinade on meat when on the grill.

1/2 cup wine vinegar

6 ounces tomato paste

FINAL barbecue coating: a commercial barbecue sauce.

2 Tbsp. lemon juice

1/4 cup Worcestershire sauce

6 Tbsp. brown sugar

1 tsp. dry mustard

1 tsp. oregano

1 tsp. salt

1/4 tsp. pepper

1 cup hot chicken bouillon

2 dashes hot sauce

Broccoli & Rice Casserole

Fairchild House, a co-op dorm at the University of Iowa, now torn down, was a haven of joy for 20 University coeds.We made our own menus and house rules and did our own housework. Each of us had a job. My job as breakfast cook was to make any and all recipes passed down from the menu committee. Making breakfast at Fairchild House was my first real cooking experience. I loved awakening as the house was sleeping, to come down the two flights of steps to the large kitchen to make breakfast. I shared a huge room with three roommates and one of my favorite recipes through the years has been this recipe of my roommate Donna Jean Furrer.

2 cups cooked rice

1/2 cup chopped celery

1/2 cup chopped onion

1/2 stick butter or
margarine

2 packages frozen
broccoli

1/2 jar cheese whiz
(small)

1 can cream of mushroom
soup

Can water chestnuts. Sliced

COOK rice and drain. Do not use Minute Rice.

SIMMER celery and onions in butter.

COOK broccoli until defrosted. Drain.

MIX altogether and bake 30 minutes at 350 degrees.

For larger quantities, add more rice and broccoli.

Brunch Eggs

Brunch eggs are a standby. Casseroles of every size and shape are made up ahead of time and frozen. Use only glass dishes to bake this scrumptious recipe. The original recipe comes from Iowa and we often call it WEDDING EGG CASSEROLE because we've made it so often for wedding breakfast receptions. It goes right from the freezer to the oven to be thawed overnight and then baked. It reheats well and lasts several days in the refrigerator. Leftovers are wonderful. If you peek into my freezer, you'll find several casseroles of all sizes labeled: Brunch eggs: Serving 2, 4 or 6.

Three dozen eggs

1/4 cup milk

1/4 pound butter

2 cans mushroom soup

2 small cans mushrooms

Mozzarella Cheese

GREASE glass baking pans.

BEAT eggs with 1/4 cup milk in blender, half of the ingredients at a time.

SCRAMBLE in half cup of butter and do use butter.

Make two layers each: Scrambled eggs
2 cans soup and the mushrooms heated together
Grated Cheese

PUT in glass dishes in a COLD oven and bake at 250 degrees for one hour.

92

Butter Mix

We serve this butter mix to guests and also put regular butter on the table. Without exception, guests prefer this lighter spread and ask for the recipe. This is a recipe from Virginia Brown and I can remember her saying, "This is so healthy for you and tastes like butter without most of the fat." This mix keeps in a crock in the refrigerator for a long time. It can be used for stovetop or oven cooking, but not for making baked goods.

2 cups butter
  (1 lb. package)

1 3/4 cup safflower oil

2 to 3 Tbsp. dry milk

2 to 3 Tbsp. wheat germ

6 Tbsp. lecithin

BEAT butter in a large mixing bowl. Add safflower oil, powdered milk, lecithin, and wheat germ.

BEAT until butter is well mixed with oil.

POUR into dish or crock and wait for it to harden in the refrigerator. Butter becomes solid when refrigerated.

93

Buttermilk Biscuits

This old-fashioned recipe is one I've made countless times. I enjoy serving these biscuits with sausage and sausage gravy. The lard and buttermilk give an exquisite taste as the flavors blend together in just the right way to bring out the bursts of flavor. Powdered buttermilk can be used if fresh buttermilk is not available.

2 cups all-purpose flour

2 tsp. baking powder

1 tsp. salt

2 Tbsp. lard

2/3 cup buttermilk

WASH hands. Mix dry ingredients in a mixing bowl. Work in lard with fingers until evenly distributed.

Quickly stir in milk with a fork, adding a little milk and then some more until dough is light and soft but not too sticky.

TURN dough out onto a floured board and knead a few strokes.

Rollout dough so it's about 3/4 inch thick.

Cut with biscuit cutter or use the floured rim of a glass.

PLACE on ungreased cookie sheet. Bake 12 to 15 minutes at 450 degrees.

94

Cabbage Salad

A long time ago, a house was built next to the marshy pond up the road from the Lazy Bee. The pond is so big it takes over an hour to walk around the craggy shoreline. The pond is harder to find now that logging has taken place around the roads to it. Every time I see a pond, it reminds me of Cabbage Salad, a jumble of many colors sparkling in the sunlight along the banks.

1/2 pound shrimp

MIX all ingredients except the ramen. Add ramen just before serving and adding the dressing.

1 small head cabbage, thinly sliced

2 green onions, chopped

1/2 cup frozen peas. thawed

2 Tbsp. toasted sesame seeds

2 Tbsp. toasted almonds, sliced

1 package top ramen, uncooked

DRESSING

2 tsp. sugar

COMBINE and shake well. Add just before serving.

1/2 cup oil

1 tsp. salt

1/2 tsp. pepper

3 Tbsp. white wine

...

Cherry Upside Down Cake

Here's an upside down cake that has a cheerful appearance because of the canned cherries. Make a double batch of sauce or s.t.r.e.t.c.h. the topping. This is as pretty as any cake you'll find on a fancy dessert tray.

1/4 cup butter

1/2 cup brown sugar

2 cans (1 pound)
   water-packed red
   sour cherries

2 tsp. grated
   lemon rind

1 cup butter
   or margarine

1 cup sugar

2 eggs

3 cups sifted flour 4

tsp. baking powder 1

tsp. salt
1 cup milk

SAUCE

4 Tbsp. sugar

4 Tbsp. cornstarch

All the juice from

the cherries

MELT *1/4* cup butter in a 9x9x2-inch pan. Sprinkle with brown sugar. Drain cherries, reserving juice. Distribute cherries evenly in the pan and add the grated lemon rind.

CREAM butter and sugar and beat in the eggs. Sift in flour, baking powder and salt. Add milk. beating until smooth. Spread over cherries. (This is not easy but if you dollop some blobs of batter at different locations, then smooth out those blobs, the sticky batter finally covers the cherries.)

BAKE in moderate 375 degree oven about 30 minutes. Cut cake in squares and top with sauce.

MAKE SAUCE: Blend sugar and cornstarch with cherry juice in a non-stick pan over medium heat.

MAKES several servings, depending upon how big you cut the squares.

Chicken/Broccoli Quiche

This comes from Barbara Thisted. It is a pie that makes its own crust. If you use fresh broccoli, steam and drain thoroughly. If you're using frozen broccoli, rinse under cold water to thaw. This will fill two 8 inch pie tins or one large 10x 1 1/2 pie plate. Once you get the hang of this and want to move on to a different ingredient, you can use ham in place of the chicken and one cup of Swiss cheese in place of the broccoli, 4 instead of 3 eggs, increase the Bisquick to 1 cup and the milk to 2 cups.

1 package of frozen broccoli (or 2 cups fresh broccoli broken into small pieces.

3 cups Cheddar cheese. shredded

1 1/2 cups chicken. cooked and cut up

2/3 cup chopped onion

1 1/3 cups milk

3 eggs

3/4 cup Bisquick baking mix

3/4 tsp. salt 1/4

tsp. pepper

GREASE pie plate.

RINSE broccoli under cold water to thaw. If broccoli is fresh. steam awhile and drain thoroughly.

MIX broccoli. 2 cups of the cheese. the chicken and onion in plate by hand.

BEAT milk. eggs. Bisquick mix, salt and pepper for 15 seconds in a blender on high or for I minute with a beater.

POUR into pie plate.

BAKE in 400 degree oven for 25 to 35 minutes or until center comes out clean.

TOP with remaining cheese and return to the hot oven and bake about 1 or 2 minutes or until the cheese melts.

COOL about five minutes and cut "into wedge shapes and serve.

Cocoa Frosting

This is the superb cocoa frosting for use on brownies or chocolate cakes. It is so creamy and easy to make, why buy canned frosting when you can make this so easily. The recipe makes 1 1/2 cups of fluffy frosting. Leftover frosting keeps a long time refrigerated. Leftovers are terrific on crackers.

2 1/2 cups sifted
  confectioners sugar

1/4 tsp. salt 1/4

Cup cocoa

1/4 cup butter or
  margarine

1/4 cup hot milk

1/2 tsp. vanilla

SIFT dry ingredients together.

CREAM butter or margarine and add part of sugar mixture alternately with the hot milk, beating until smooth.

ADD vanilla, mixing in well.

98

Coconut Bars

It was through the University of Iowa's placement office that my college roommate, Sally, and I found summer jobs as waitresses miles away at Gratiot Inn Resort on Lake Michigan. From the East Coast came guys from Harvard and Yale to be bus boys and from Iowa came Sally and Jo Ann. Little did we know that we were to perform on Wednesday and Sunday nights for the guests. It was perform or go back to Iowa so I created a hat revue for the waiters and waitresses. The Crazy Hat show was a hit, much as these cookie bars sent to a girl named June from her Mom.

1/2 cup spry or
    margarine

1/2 tsp. salt

1/2 cup brown sugar

1 cup flour

2 eggs, beaten

1 cup brown sugar

1 tsp. vanilla

2 Tbsp. flour mixed
    with 1/2 tsp. baking
    powder

1 1/2 cups coconut

1 cup coarsely cut nuts

COMBINE fat and salt. Add sugar and cream well. Add flour. Spread this mixture in a greased 9 by 12 inch pan. Bake in slow oven about 20 minutes at 300 degrees.

To the beaten eggs, which have been beaten quite thick, add the sugar, vanilla, flour, baking powder, coconut and nuts.

SPREAD over the baked mixture and return to oven and bake for 20 to 25 minutes. Cool and cut in small bars.

Crazy Cake

Mother baked this muddy, moist cake, still fresh in taste and texture after a week has gone by. It is made of ingredients normally found in any kitchen, with exception, perhaps, of the lard and cocoa. The cake is ready to eat after it has cooled slightly. The taste becomes richer and more moist as the days pass.

1 cup sugar

1 egg

1/2 cup milk

1/2 cup cocoa

1/2 cup lard (don't use substitute)

1/2 tsp. salt

1 tsp. baking powder

1/2 tsp. soda

1 tsp. vanilla

1 1/2 cups flour 1/2 Cup boiling water

PUT ingredients in a large mixing bowl in the order given. Add boiling water and *then* stir together.

BEAT for three minutes.

POUR into a nine-inch, greased and floured pan.

BAKE in a slow oven (325 degrees) for about 30 to 35 minutes or until a toothpick comes out clean from the center.

Fabulous Flan

After Lazy Bee guests have had a tour and settled into their quarters, we often present a Fiesta menu. First there's a layered dip with chips and salsa. Then, quesadillas hot from the griddle. Then, enchiladas that are accompanied by a zesty garden salad. Then follows this Fabulous Flan that's been prepared in advance. It's a pleasant, easy to make dessert. Caramelizing the sugar is fun. The hot liquid turns into the coating for the custard.

1 3/4 cups sugar

3 egg whites

8 egg yolks

2 cans evaporated milk

2 tsp. vanilla

MELT one cup sugar over very low heat. Pour into an 8 x 10 pan or 2 loaf pans, tilting the hot liquid so it coats bottom and a little of the sides. Allow to cool. (HINT: If sugar is too slow to begin to liquefy, turn up heat slowly. This may take 20 minutes or more to bring to the liquid stage.)

BEAT egg whites and yolks together. Add milk, the remaining 3/4 cup sugar and the vanilla.

POUR in the sugar-lined pans.

PLACE pans in a larger pan with about an inch of water in a 350 degree oven for about 1 1/4 hour or until a knife inserted in the center comes out clean.

COOL. Turn onto a plate while still warm. Refrigerate several hours before serving. Serves 10 to 12.

Flavorful Onion Soup

When I returned to Iowa after my first visit to Paris, I tried recreating this soup which is a meal-in-itself. The cafe where I ate was one of those romantic little places stepped down into from the sidewalk, with immaculate white tablecloths and ever present waiters. When I was trying out several onion soup recipes, Mother happened to be visiting and she finally asked, "Do you have onion soup EVERY night?" This recipe is the end result of attempting to put together. a soup from which you PULL up cheese from the bottom of the dish, a soup which brings together in equal amounts the bread/cheese/liquid.

2 pounds yellow onions, pealed and sliced thin

2 Tbsp. vegetable oil

1 clove garlic, crushed

1 tsp. salt 3

Tbsp. flour
8 cups or seven 10 1/2 ounce cans condensed beef broth. heated

Toasted slices. of French bread

3/4 cup Gruyere cheese

Parmesan cheese

SEPARATE onion slices into rings.

SAUTE in oil the garlic clove and onions. Sprinkle with salt and stir often and gently until they are light brown. Use a heavy four-to-five quart saucepan or soup kettle over a moderate heat.

ONIONS are done when they are a rich, golden brown.

SPRINKLE them with flour and stir again and cook for another 2 to 3 minutes.

ADD hot broth. Bring to boil, then simmer over low heat for 30 to 40 minutes. Skim off fat occasionally. Taste for seasoning and add more salt if needed.

From a loaf of French bread, cut thick slices and bake in preheated 300 degree oven on baking sheet. Brush with olive oil, turn and bake another 15 minutes. Bread should be lightly browned. When ready to serve, bring soup to boil and put piece of bread in each serving bowl, sprinkling with Parmesan cheese and a layer of Gruyere cheese, adding soup and topping with Parmesan cheese. Put in hot 475 degree oven until cheese melts. SERVE.

French Bread

My Granddaughter Anna and I began baking this bread together when she was three years old. It has five ingredients, plus one other which is used to coat the bread before putting it in the oven. The thought of this recipe brings up memories of a little girl peeking under a moist towel to see if the bread had risen. Kneading bread feels almost as good as eating the hot bread just out of the oven. If you make half a recipe, still use two packets of dry yeast. Makes six French-type long loaves.

2 Tbsp. dry yeast
(2 packets)

5 cups warm water

4 Tbsp. sugar

2 Tbsp. salt

14 cups white flour

2 egg whites, beaten
with fork

PUT yeast in large bowl. Add warm water and stir until dissolved.

ADD sugar, salt and flour and knead 10 minutes or count 200 kneading actions. Put in margarine-coated bowl and cover with a towel wrung out in hot water. Let rise in as warm a spot as you can find.

Let rise until doubled. Punch down and knead three or four times to remove air. Divide into 6 parts. Shape into long, thin loaves and put on two well greased cookie sheets. Slash tops with sharp knife. Brush with two egg whites.

LET rise again.

BAKE 15 minutes in preheated 450 degree oven, then for 30 minutes at 350. Remove from pans and cool on racks. Wrap in foil if freezing. To serve after the bread comes from freezer, warm in foil for 20 minutes.

Frozen Cheese Cake

Jo Patterson is one of the great cooks of the South. During a family vacation in Orlando, when the children were on college spring break, Jo made recipes like this. After a day of sightseeing, we sat down at her beautifully set table, relaxed and enjoyed banquet after banquet. John Patterson squeezed grapefruit juice for us from their heavily-laden backyard tree for beverages. Talk about Southern hospitality. This was it. Even to the nicest thing to say as we were leaving. Jo said, "This has been wonderful, but we'll be so sad because the party's over."

10 ounces cottage cheese

MIX cottage and cream cheeses together.

2 packages cream cheese (8 oz.)

ADD egg yolks beaten with sugar. Add cream which has been whipped stiff.

4 eggs separated

1 cup whipping cream

FOLD in beaten egg whites and vanilla.

1 tsp. vanilla

1 cup sugar

LINE two ice cube trays with crumbs, filling with cheese mixture and cover with crumbs. Freeze. Unfreeze when ready to serve and add topping if desired.

Graham crackers, crushed

STRAWBERRY GLAZE

2 cups strawberries

MASH berries with sugar and let stand 30 minutes. Mix with cornstarch and cook until thick and clear. Strain and cool. Pour over berries and refrigerate.

1/2 cup sugar

2 Tbsp. cornstarch

104

Frozen Fruit Salad

When we are having a spell of hot weather, endless days when it doesn't cool off at night as it usually does in the summer, and when everyone is a little off key, this is a perfect time to make a frozen fruit salad. This is a salad where each bite is like chewing into a fruity-ice crystal piece of fruit like strawberry or pineapple. A frozen salad can return a mood of testiness to one of harmony.

1 can of canned apricots. cut and drained

2 packages frozen strawberries

1 large can pineapple tidbits, drained

4 bananas. diced

Enough water to make 1 cup liquid

1/2 cup sugar

MIX drained fruits. Stir juice from the apricots and pineapple and add enough water to make one cup of liquid.

ADD 1/2 cup of sugar. Bring to boil. Cool. Then. pour over fruit.

FREEZE in 9 x 13 inch pan. Cut into squares and serve on lettuce leaves.

German Potato Pancakes

A rare and special treat for as long as Bud remembers is this dish. Grating potatoes and onions is hard work so it's, "I'll grate if you cook." Although this is a meal in itself, potato pancakes can be accompanied by applesauce and German sausage or broiled trout. We like to make extra to freeze and warm up later for breakfast. They also fry up like hash browns.

8 potatoes, raw

1 large onion

5 egg whites, stiffly beaten

1 Tbsp. salt

1/2 tsp. pepper

1 Tbsp. celery seed

1 clove garlic

1/4 cup flour

Crisco, for frying

PEEL potatoes. If you leave about 10 percent of the skins on, it improves the flavor.

Coarsely grate potatoes into a large bowl. Peel and grate onion into bowl. Try to keep tears out of bowl.

SEPARATE eggs, dropping yokes into bowl with spuds. Whip whites until very stiff. Fold together with spuds and season.

ADD just enough flour to soak up water from potatoes. Drop batter into large frying pan with HOT butter-flavored Crisco.

FRY until browned on both sides.

Gingerbread

Gingerbread is just like the little girl with the curl right in the middle of her forehead. When it's good, it's very, very good and when it's bad, it's just horrid. This recipe makes a mellow, mild-tasting bread, good hot or cold. Gingerbread can stand alone as an afternoon snack or welcome-home treat after a cross-country ski trek.

3/4 cup molasses

1/2 cup boiling water

MELT and blend molasses, water, sugar, and butter over low heat. Stir constantly.

3/4 cup sugar

1/2 cup melted butter
or margarine

Remove from stove. Add egg, then the cinnamon, cloves, nutmeg, soda and flour.

1 egg

MIX well. Bake in an 8 x 8 inch pan, two inches deep, which has been greased and floured.

3/4 tsp. cinnamon

BAKE for 30 minutes in a 350 degree oven.

1/2 tsp. cloves

1/2 tsp. nutmeg

1 level tsp. soda

1 1/2 cups sifted
White flour

107

Glazed, Fresh Peach Pie

Peaches, juicy, succulent peaches are grown in Washington. For this fresh, peach pie, cut them in half and arrange in an unbaked pastry shell after the bottom of the shell has been sprinkled thickly with mixture of sugar and flour. Remaining flour-sugar mixture is sprinkled over peaches, butter is dotted on, and a few dashes of cinnamon are added to enhance the flavor.

Six to eight fresh peaches

PEEL fresh peaches, then cut them into halves.

1 nine-inch pastry shell

1 cup sugar

MEASURE flour into small mixing bowl and combine with sugar. Sprinkle 3/4's of this mixture into bottom of unbaked pastry shell.

2 Tbsp. flour

2 Tbsp. butter

Few dashes cinnamon

PLACE peach halves upside down in the pie shell and sprinkle remaining mixture over top of peaches. Dot on butter, then sprinkle cinnamon lightly over all.

BAKE in 400 degree oven for 10 minutes, after which heat is reduced to 375 degrees and baking continued for another 45 minutes or until fruit is glazed and crust is browned.

Graham Cracker Torte

Everyone makes a dish that no one seems to make as well. That's the case with this recipe. But, fortunately, this dessert turns out special even though Irene Packey hasn't made it for years. At the age of 90, she quit cooking, got married and goes out to eat. Serve this with whipped cream or dessert topping to blend the flavors of. the graham crackers, pudding and the graham cracker topping. This is a Swedish dessert, passed down through three generations.

22 graham crackers
(11 double)

1/4 cup sugar

1 tsp. cinnamon
(heaping)

4 tsp. melted butter

Filling

4 egg yolks or 2
whole eggs

1/2 cup sugar

3 Tbsp. flour

2 cups milk

1/8 tsp. salt

1 tsp. vanilla

ROLL crackers fine. Add sugar, cinnamon and melted butter and mix altogether.

PAT half the mixture in the bottom of an 8x8 pan and save the rest for the top.

MIX eggs, sugar, flour, milk, salt and vanilla in a non-stick pan or in the top of a double boiler. (Use a whisk to mix and stir.) Cook until slightly thick.

POUR filling over the mixture in pan and top with rest of crackers.

Bake 20 minutes in a 325 degree oven. Serve hot or cold.

Ham On Top Stove

Bud's Aunt Isabelle Brost of Chicago has several claims to fame. In addition to raising her sister's four children who were orphaned at early ages, she has an uncanny sense for making smart investment choices and for coming up with this method of baking ham on top a stove so that it is tender and moist. Once smitten with her way of boiling a ham in water, we have stove-topped hams ever since. Then, we reheat any ham that's left over in plastic packets in water on top the stove. Often we save the water and use it to make pea soup.

3/4 pot of water

8 1b. shank end ham

Several bay leaves

Dozen whole cloves

4 to 8 chunks of onion. cut in large pieces

2 cloves garlic. cut into slices

Celery tops with leaves

3 Tbsp. dry mustard

PUT water in soup pot so that it covers ham and is about 3/4 full.

ADD ham and seasonings.

BRING to boil. Simmer for an hour and a half.

Turn off burner. Let ham sit in the pot for another hour and a half before serving.

Honey-Glazed Carrots

Living year-round in the mountains takes guts, tradable skills, and tenacity. Our neighbor a mile up on Stone Mountain trades his mechanical skills, backhoe work and storable items like potatoes from his organic garden at the Barter Faire. B.Z. promised me a load of peat from his garden so I can raise carrots like he does and make them into this dish.

5 medium carrots. peeled

1/3 cup water

1/4 tsp. salt 2

Tbsp. honey

2 tsp. lemon juice

1/4 tsp. ground cinnamon

CUT carrots into 1/2 inch slices.

COMBINE carrots, water, and salt in a small saucepan.

Cook until carrots are crisp and tender. Drain.

COMBINE carrots, honey, lemon juice, and ground cinnamon in a small saucepan. Cook over medium heat, stirring gently until carrots are glazed.

Huevoes Rancheros

Bud orders huevos rancheros at restaurants around the country just to see what they come up with. Some of the strangest concoctions have been found in the South. This is our favorite recipe for making Huevoes and is an adaptation of a recipe made by his brother, Geno, a charter yacht captain in the Virgin Islands. Crisp shells are smothered with warmed beans and grated cheese, warmed in the oven, and topped with a fried egg. We put out shredded lettuce, chopped tomatoes, and salsa as accompaniments.

6 corn tortillas

1 can refried beans

2 cups grated cheese *

2 cups lettuce chopped

1 cup roasted green chilies

6 fresh eggs

(*In order of preference:
Longhorn
Monterey Jack
Cheddar
Mozzarella)

FRY tortillas until crisp in hot oil. Drain on paper towels.   Keep warm in oven.

HEAT beans with two tablespoons of oil left over from frying tortillas. Spread beans in a thin or thick layer on tortillas.

COVER tortilla shell with grated cheese and melt in 300 degree oven.

As cheese is melting in warm oven, fry eggs to taste. Plop an egg on each tortilla and serve.

(Serves six at Hillside House and two at the lazy Bee.)

Huguenot Torte

I met Jackie, who was from North Carolina; when we were at Perrin Air Force Base, Texas, in the early '50's. Jackie made this. showy dessert, liked by all ages, and so nice for occasions when you want something flashy without spending a lot of time or money. This dessert has been baked for baby showers, bridal parties, and Rose Bowl gatherings. Squirt with dessert topping from the can or use real whipped cream. Line the oven with foil as the torte can ooze over the top of the baking dish.

4 eggs

3 cups sugar

8 Tbsp. flour

5 tsp. baking
powder

2 cups chopped tart
cooking apples

2 cups chopped
pecans or walnuts

BEAT whole eggs with electric mixer or rotary beater until very frothy and lemon-colored.

Add rest of ingredients. Pour into two well-buttered baking pans about 8 x 12 x 1 or two inches. Bake in 325 degree oven about 45 minutes or until crusty and brown.

TO SERVE: scoop up with pancake turner and keep crusty part on top. Pile onto plates and cover with whipped cream or ice cream.

Lazy "B" Sugar Cookies

These sugar cookies are lusciously rich. The dough is perfect to cut into holiday shapes and sizes. The finished cookies, frosted or unfrosted, look pretty on a plate. We roll out a lot of these at the Lazy Bee and Hillside House. You'll want to pass a plateful of sugar cookies to guests, too. The way I roll out cookies, this recipes makes about 50 large ones.

1/2 cup butter or margarine	CREAM butter.
1 cup sugar	BEAT in sugar, egg, cream or milk, and vanilla.
2 eggs	ADD flour, salt and baking powder sifted together. Mix well.
1 Tbsp. cream or milk	ROLL out dough on a floured surface and cut into shapes.
1/2 tsp. vanilla	
1 1/2 cups sifted flour	BAKE about 8 minutes at 375 degrees. Makes 50 to 60.
1/4 tsp. salt	
1 tsp. baking powder	

Mexican Layered Dip

When we bring an hors d'oeuvre to a party, we like to take this dip. Bud, who is an engineer, is very logical. One of his observations was that, at a party, Mexican dip is always first to go. It's easy to put together and makes a pretty presentation, the beans showing up around the edge, sour cream placed in the center, the chunks of green, chopped avocados and red tomatoes placed around the sour cream.

2 cans of plain chili

1/2 pound processed
cheese spread. cubed

1 cup .sour cream

2 Tbsp. green onion
slices

1 cup chopped tomato

1 avocado. chopped in
chunks

Lime or lemon juice

COMBINE chili and processed cheese in saucepan. Stir over low heat until cheese spread is melted.

POUR into 10x16 inch dish and center with sour cream.

SURROUND sour cream with chopped tomato and avocado chunks which have been dipped in lime or lemon juice. Sprinkle chopped green onions around the edges.

Monday Night Meatloaf

Monday night. It must be meatloaf for dinner. Monday is the only night I have a pre-set entree. Of course, you can add many additional ingredients to meatloaf, such as catsup, spices, even applesauce, but this is the way I've put meatloaf together through the years and it has always turned out moist and non-fail.

1 or 1 1/2 pounds
  hamburger

1 large onion

2 eggs

1/2 cup milk

1 cup bread crumbs

1 tsp. salt

1/2 tsp. pepper

MIX hamburger, chopped onion, 2 eggs, milk, breadcrumbs, and seasonings.

USING clean hands, mix altogether.

PLACE in greased baking dish and bake at 350 degrees.

Old Fashioned Egg Nog

This is a mighty fine beverage for the holiday season. It makes a thick drink. It's very rich and almost as luxurious to look at as it is to taste. Make it several days in advance so it can mellow.

12 egg yolks

1 1/2 cups sugar

1/4 tsp~ salt

12 egg whites

1 quart heavy cream.
    beaten

1 quart milk

1 quart bourbon
  whiskey

1 cup rum

BEAT egg yolks with one cup sugar and the salt until very light.

BEAT whites until stiff and beat in 1/2 cup sugar. (Use an electric mixer.)

COMBINE yolk mixture and egg white mixture and beat until thoroughly blended.

BEAT in cream, then milk. Stir in whiskey. Beat well. Add rum.

POUR into containers and store in a cool place.

SHAKE well before using. Sprinkle with nutmeg.

Orange Salad

Bud and I were married in an Episcopal outdoors along the banks of the Pend Oreille River. Guests brought potluck dishes instead of gifts. Here's a recipe for a salad that someone brought for our Memorial Day ceremony in 1985:

1 large package jello

2 cups hot boiling water

2 packages of 8-ounce cream cheese

3 cups mini marshmallows

SOFTEN cheese in large bowl and set aside.

PLACE gelatin in large bowl and mix with boiling water.

Using an electric mixer, add small amounts of hot gelatin to cream cheese and mix until creamy.

Keep adding gelatin to cheese until blended.

Quickly add marshmallows while mixture is hot. Mix until salad is smooth.

REFRIGERATE.

Pineapple Upside Down Cake

This old favorite has been served to many guests and has been taken to lots of Cub Scout Pack meetings and church potlucks. It makes a perfect afternoon snack or grand finale for a dinner party. It looks pretty on a serving plate, the brown topping covering the yellow pineapple rings, and the red cherries peeping through.

1/3 cup butter

1/2 cup ,firmly packed brown sugar

1 *(20* ounce) can sliced pineapple, drained

Maraschino cherries

Pecan halves

1 1/3 cups sifted flour

1 cup sugar

2 tsp. baking powder

1/2 tsp. salt

1/3 cup soft shortening

2/3 cup milk

1 tsp. vanilla

1/2 tsp. lemon flavoring

1 egg

MELT butter in heavy 10-inch skillet or put melted butter in round baking dish.

SPREAD brown sugar evenly over butter and arrange pineapple slices in attractive pattern on top sugar. Put a cherry in the center of each slice and fill in spaces with pecan halves.

COMBINE flour, sugar, baking powder and salt in mixing bowl. Add shortening, milk and flavorings. Beat 2 minutes at medium speed with electric mixer or 300 vigorous strokes by hand. Add egg and beat two more minutes scraping bowl frequently.

POUR batter over fruit and bake at 350 degrees for 40 to 50 minutes or until cake tests done with a toothpick pulled out clean.

TURN upside down onto a plate big enough to hold the cake.

Pounded Beef or Venison

As managing editor of the Florissant Valley Reporter, I wrote articles, features, editorials, covered meetings, and wrote an occasional food column. This recipe is from a mother of 12 who said she could stretch a small amount of meat to serve her large family. I especially like the part where you pound the round beef steak (or venison) out flat with a hammer. I also like seeing the meat puff up as it quickly sears in the pot. The meat is tender enough to cut with a fork. This is especially good for venison.

Large round steak, about 1/8 to 1/4 inch thick

Or. use venison

Oil

Flour

Water

Salt

REMOVE any membrane and fat from meat. Cut into palm-sized pieces.

WASH off head of a hammer and pound the meat pieces out flat on a cutting board.

PUT some flour in a flat dish and coat the pieces. Put a few tablespoons of vegetable oil in a large pot.   Put in the floured meat pieces and watch them puff up and grow in size.

When they have browned in a few minutes, remove the pieces to a platter. Add a few tablespoons of flour to remaining meat drippings and enough water to make gravy. Salt lightly. Put meat pieces back in the pan with the gravy and simmer.

This can be made ahead and reheated. It can sit merrily upon the stove waiting upon someone who is late.

Quick Pork Chop Casserole

Every time I make this quick pork chop recipe, it brings to mind the technique of one of my St. Louis neighbors who used to rush in the door late and put a slice of onion on a cookie sheet in the oven. This aroma soon filled the air, leading her family to believe dinner was underway, as she read the mail and collected her thoughts. Later, she would prepare this quick pork chop casserole to satisfy everyone.

3/4 cup raw rice

PUT rice in greased casserole dish. Empty the can of soup and put the raw pork chops on top.

Can mushroom soup

Several raw pork chops

SPRINKLE with water chestnuts.

3/4 cup water

POUR 3/4's can of water (using the soup can) over the pork chops.

Few water chestnuts, cut up

BAKE 1 1/2 hour at 325 degrees.

Rhubarb Muffins

In the summer, home economics students at the University of Northern Iowa offered cooking courses to the community. Presentations by the students were quite creative. I remember this recipe because one student pretended to cut up another student who was dressed like a stalk of rhubarb. Muffins are moist and tangy due to the tartness of the buttermilk. Use either fresh or canned buttermilk.

1 1/4 cups brown sugar

1/2 cup vegetable oil

1 egg

2 tsp. vanilla

1 cup buttermilk

1 1/2 cups diced rhubarb

1/2 cup chopped nuts

2 1/2 cups flour

1 tsp. baking powder

1 tsp. baking soda
1/2 tsp. salt

1/3 cup sugar

1 tsp. cinnamon

1 Tbsp. melted butter

COMBINE brown sugar, oil, egg and vanilla.

BEAT until blended and stir in buttermilk, rhubarb and nuts.

COMBINE flour, baking powder, baking soda and salt and add all at once to the rhubarb mixture. Stir just until mixed.

FILL paper-lined muffin tins a scant 2/3's full. Combine sugar, cinnamon and butter and sprinkle over the batter, pressing topping in slightly.

BAKE at 400 degrees .for 20 minutes. Makes about 24 muffins.

Scalloped Turkey

As a young Air Force wife, I wrote articles for a Texas newspaper. Even then, as a budding cook, I was beginning this collection of American basics. This was the result of one of my features for the <u>Denison Herald.</u> It's a fine recipe to make after cooking a turkey. It makes a large, filling casserole for a crowd. Quick and easy, it's also very economical. Can be frozen.

1 pint cubed turkey chunks	Place turkey chunks in buttered 9 x 12 baking dish.
1 pint turkey broth	
2 Tbsp. flour	Make gravy from broth, flour and shortening.
2 Tbsp. shortening	Mix remaining ingredients together lightly. Spread dressing
3 cups bread crumbs	mixture evenly over the turkey chunks and pour gravy over the
1/3 cup melted butter	top.
I tsp. powdered sage	Bake in 350 degree oven about 30 minutes until cooked through and
1/4 cup milk	lightly browned.
1/4 tsp. salt	Cut in squares and garnish with parsley if desired. Serve with
1 Tbsp. chopped onion	mashed potatoes.

Slush

Slush makes a large amount of beverage, perhaps enough for 30 persons, and can be used for a dinner party, a reception or wherever a slushy drink seems appropriate. Add a carbonated or not. Bud likes it carbonated for an extra fizz. We made up Slush for a friend's 50th wedding reception. A bartender was there, too. But most folks opted for this Slush.

3 cups water

4 green tea bags

Boil three cups of water and add the four green tea bags. (Black tea can be used without a noticeable difference.) Cool.

7 more cups water

2 cups sugar

Boil seven cups of water with two cups of sugar and combine the two water mixtures.

1 can (12 oz.) orange juice

ADD orange juice and frozen lemonade pulp. Stir well. Then add one cup vodka or gin.

1 can (12 oz.) frozen lemonade

Vodka or gin

START freezing mixture in containers, allowing about a half inch at the top of each container.

AFTER five hours or so have passed, stir mixture again and add another cup of vodka or gin. After the mixture freezes awhile, it is ready to serve. Use 1/2 slush mixture and add 7 up if desired.

Sour Cream Apple Pie

Washington is the nation's leading apple producer. We follow the ups and downs of the apple industry, and hope the orchards keep up the supply, for they are a key ingredients in many of our recipes. We love to serve this regional fruit and often bake an apple pie. We especially like this recipe.

1 uncooked 9-inch
pie shell

4 cups apples, peeled
and sliced

1/4 tsp. salt

2 Tbsp. flour

2 Tbsp. fresh lemon juice

1/2 cup sugar

1 egg

1/2 pint sour cream

11/2 cup brown
sugar

3 Tbsp. melted butter

1 tsp. cinnamon

PEEL, core and thinly slice apples. Place into an unbaked pie shell.

MIX salt, flour, lemon juice, sugar and egg. Add sour cream and pour over apples.

BAKE in pre-heated 400 degree oven for 15 minutes. While the pie is baking, mix brown sugar, butter and cinnamon with fork to make crumbs for the topping.

AFTER removing pie from oven, put on topping and then return to oven and bake for another 35 minutes at 350 degrees.

Stir-Fried Green Beans

We came across this method of cooking fresh green beans when we raised a garden in Iowa's rich black soil, so rich anyone, even an inexperienced or inept gardener, could be successful. The first step in making these beans is to slice them on the bias in strips. This shortens the cooking time. Beans turn out soft with a lingering hint of crispness.

5 cups green beans, about one pound

SLICE beans on the bias in strips of about 1/8 inch.

3 Tbsp. cooking oil

ADD oil to heated heavy skillet or wok. and heat.

1/4 cup sliced onions
1 tsp. chicken bouillon
   granules

1/2 tsp. salt

ADD beans and stir about three minutes. Then, add remaining ingredients, taking pan off stove if you haven't prepared and measured ingredients before starting to cook.

1/2 cup water

REDUCE heat to medium, cover and cook beans until tendercrisp, about five minutes.

Strawberry Jam

My version of heaven is fields of strawberries or patches of raspberries to pick. There will be buckets available and friends who like to go along berry picking. There's nothing worse than a grumbling berry picker. Perhaps there is something historically present in genes of people who love to pick berries. The first time I saw the blackberry bushes growing wild in Oregon, I thought I'd died and gone to heaven. Most Oregonians consider them weeds, but that leaves more blackberries for folks like us to pick. We go huckleberry picking on Huckleberry Mountain near Meadow Lake.

3 cups sugar

3 cups whole strawberries

PLACE strawberries in heavy four or five quart saucepan.

PUT sugar in center but do not stir.

USE low heat and simmer half an hour or until sugar is absorbed.

POUR into a heavy bowl and let set overnight.

PUT into hot sterilized jars and pour melted paraffin over jam.

Turkey Soup

When Bud gets ready to make soup, he plans to have lots of onions and celery on hand. When the turkey is just out of the oven and being carved for the table, the carcass and bones are thrown into a 15-quart soup pot, half filled with water, or enough to cover the bones, and simmered over night or throughout the next day. This recipe is for a large turkey. Reduce ingredients for a smaller bird.

12 quarts water

Carcass and bones from
20 lb. turkey

2 onions, chopped

Whole bunch celery
with tops

Salt or salt substitute
to taste

Pepper to taste

Sage

Paprika

1 cup rice or 1 package
16-ounce wide noodles
(either but not both) not
cooked

PULL bones out of the pot which has been simmering over night.and the following morning.   Remove meat from bones and put the meat back in the pot.

You can cook rice or noodles separately before straining and adding them to the pot.

ADD onions and celery, chopped, and simmer until they are cooked through, about 20 minutes.

ADD spices by the half tablespoonful until you get the taste of the soup just right.

128

Waldorf Salad

Waldorf is a favorite salad in the state of Washington where apples are so ABUNDANT. We see apples being sold on street corners and by roadsides, in stores, and driveways of houses even have signs out in front. This salad makes a fine companion to a simple lunch of soup and a sandwich, or it looks festive on the more elegant table. The brilliant red apples in this salad can highlight a holiday meal.

2 large apples

2/3 cup finely cut
   celery

5 tsp. mayonnaise

1/4tsp. nutmeg

1/4 tsp. salt

1/2 Tbsp. lemon juice

1/2 cup walnut meats

Lettuce leaves

CUT apples, peeled or not, your preference, into small even cubes.

Into each cup of cut apples, add 2/3 cup finely cut celery and five tsp of mayonnaise. Mix well.

ADD nutmeg, salt and lemon juice.

SPRINKLE walnut meats on top the mixture upon lettuce leaves.

Index

Index

Index